FRONTIERS OF FORTUNE
The Fur Trade

TRADE ROUTES SERIES
*Prepared under the general editorship
of Edward R. Sammis*

FRONTIERS
OF FORTUNE
THE FUR TRADE

by DONALD HONIG

McGRAW-HILL BOOK COMPANY
New York · Toronto · London · Sydney

Woodcuts by Alexander Anderson appearing on pages 10, 15, 22, 79, 108
Courtesy of Prints Division, The New York Public Library, Astor, Lenox and Tilden Foundations

Picture appearing on page 96
Courtesy of Culver Pictures, Inc.

Pictures appearing on pages 14, 17, 21, 23, 25, 29, 43, 63, 98, 103, 105, 107, 109, 118, 126
Courtesy of The Granger Collection

Pictures appearing on pages 21, 55, 70, 73, 75, 82, 83, 87, 88, 92, 95, 111, 123
Courtesy of the Hudson's Bay Company

Pictures appearing on pages 11, 24, 31, 36–37, 48–49
Courtesy of the I. N. Phelps Stokes Collection of American Historical Prints, Prints Division, The New York Public Library

Pictures appearing on pages 2, 18–19, 30, 80, 99, 101, 114, 115, 120, 124
Reproduced from the Collections of The Library of Congress

Pictures appearing on pages 8, 13, 32, 64, 66, 69, 85, 91
Courtesy of the Minnesota Historical Society

Picture appearing on page 76
Courtesy of the Museum of the American Indian, Heye Foundation

Art reproduced on page 77
Located in the Royal Ontario Museum

Picture appearing on page 33
Courtesy of the Yale University Library

Picture appearing on the jacket
Courtesy of the Public Archives of Canada

Drawings by Don Ogilvie appear on pages 20, 38, 52, 58, 84, 115

Library of Congress Catalog Card Number: 67-24953.

*For Jed
and Johanna*

CONTENTS

Pierre Radisson (standing) and Medard Groseilliers travel north.

Radisson Shames
the Braves

It was the year 1656. A chilly spring breeze was blowing the needles of the pine trees on Prairie Island in the Mississippi River. Standing alone under the clear blue sky, facing 500 stoic Huron Indians, was twenty-one-year-old Pierre Radisson, a French youth already hardened by his months of adventure in the wilderness of North America.

Young Radisson, dressed as the Hurons were in the skins of deer and beaver, and with a knife wedged into his belt, was staring boldly at the Indians who were sitting around him in an enormous circle.

That morning the chiefs had told Radisson that they refused to accompany him and his brother-in-law, Medard Chouart Groseilliers, to Quebec. The hundreds of canoes piled high with beaver pelts would remain right there unless he could make them change their minds. The pelts were the fruits of nearly two perilous and strenuous years —including two brutal winters—that the Frenchmen had spent with the Indians, trapping beaver in what are now the states of Wisconsin and Minnesota.

Without the help of their Indian friends they could never undertake the 2,000-mile, seven-week journey back east. Radisson knew what was troubling the Hurons: the bloodthirsty Iroquois—the same Iroquois who had driven the Hurons from their villages along the St. Lawrence River.

American Indians wore and traded furs.

In all likelihood they would be lying in ambush somewhere along the precarious route to Quebec.

The Hurons had great respect for Radisson. They watched him now as he gazed steadily over the waters. For a long time he stood motionless, caught up in his thoughts. Then his eyes roved across the red and black painted faces around him.

"Who am I?" he said suddenly, lashing out at them in their own language, which he knew well. "Am I a foe or a friend? If I am a foe, why did you suffer me to live so long among you? If I am a friend, and if you take me so to be, listen to what I shall say. You know that I hazarded my life traveling far and wide with you, and that we have endured much together."

The Indians sat wordlessly in their great circle, smoking their pipes, their unwinking eyes fixed upon the solitary man in their midst.

The young Frenchman's eyes grew contemptuous now, as he observed their faces. He noted their deerskin breeches, the beaver skins draped around their shoulders. He looked at the necklaces and porcelain bracelets which they had received from him in trade and of which they were so proud.

Radisson understood the Hurons' fear. They believed themselves defenseless against Iroquois attack. But he knew how to play on this fear.

"Stay here," he shouted at them, "and you will see the enemy set upon you. You will be like beavers in a trap. How will you defend yourselves? How will you defend your villages, your wives, your children—with beaver skins?"

Suddenly the speaker made a dramatic and daring gesture. He snatched the beaver pelt from the shoulders of a young brave standing before him and began striking him with it, showing how ineffectual the "weapon" was. The Indian glared at Radisson, but did not retaliate.

"Won't your enemy gloat when you perish without defending yourselves!" Radisson threw the robe down. "Do you not know the French way? We are used to fighting with arms—not robes. Do you think the French will come to your aid when most of you have been slain by your own fault? You know that they cannot come up without you. Shall they come to baptize your dead? Shall your children learn to be slaves among the Iroquois for their fathers' cowardice?"

Radisson paused; his words hovered in the air. He still had his trump card, one final word, with which he hoped to shame the reluctant Hurons into joining him.

Quebec was a proud city in the 17th century.

QUEBEC, *The Capital of* NEW-FRANCE, *a Bishoprick, and Seat of the Soverain Court.*

1. The Citadel. 2. the Castle.	7. Cathedral of Our Lady.	14. The Bishop's House. 15. The
3. Magazine. 4. y̆ Recolets.	8. The Palace 9. y̆ Seminary. 11. S.t Charles River.	Parish Church of the Lower Town. 16. The Upper Town v. y̆ Lower Town.
5. Ursulines. 6. Jesuits. 7.	10. The Hôtel Dieu.	12. The Common Hospital. 13. The Hermitage of the Recolets. 18. The Platform & Battery of Cannon. 19. The Isle of Orleans. 20. Point Lievi.

Pierre Radisson opened new fur routes for both the French and the English.

"For mine own part," he cried, "I will venture, choosing to die like a man rather than to live like a beggar. Having not wherewithal to defend myself, farewell; I have my sack of corn ready. Take all my pelts. I shall live without you."

He then strode boldly from the meeting, accompanied by Groseilliers. The two Frenchmen retired to a spot under a bluff. There they stood under the trees and watched the Indians' reaction.

Radisson brooded as he watched, impatient and determined. Like all great pioneers he was a dreamer—and his dream that day was to get his cargo of beaver pelts to Quebec. It was important not only to him but to France, for the battle lines for possession of the North American continent were being drawn between the French and the British in that year, 1656. The nation that controlled the riches of the fur trade was going to go a long way toward winning that battle. Radisson wanted to get back not only with his pelts, but also with the information he had obtained concerning the location of fur animals, waterways, and possible trade routes. Radisson and Groseilliers had been the first white men to reach the upper waters of the river the Indians called *Misi Sipi*—the great river.

For a long time the Hurons sat and talked among themselves. Occasionally the talk became heated. The Frenchmen heard the rising voices, watched the animated armwaving. Several of the chiefs stood up and raised their beaver skins over their heads, then threw them to the ground. Others picked up the dropped skins and shook them in the faces of the throwers.

At last several of the chiefs separated themselves from the group. They came over to where Radisson was waiting. The Frenchman recorded their words in his memoirs:

"We see that you are in the right; the voyage is not broken. The young people took it very ill that you have beaten them with a skin. All avowed to die like men and undertake the journey."

Radisson, delighted, grasped their hands and told them to begin preparations to depart.

Several days went by. The Hurons built elevated sides of dried beaver skins above the gunwales of the canoes to protect themselves from enemy arrows. They laid aboard nets for fishing, and ample stores of dried corn. Radisson was ready to embark for Quebec with his precious cargo and his equally valuable information.

The convoy journeyed across Lake Superior, through the channel at Sault Ste. Marie, and over the northern end of Lake Huron to Georgian Bay. From there they portaged (carried their canoes overland) to Lake Nipissing and shot the Ottawa River rapids.

The journey went smoothly until they reached the lower part of the Ottawa. This was Iroquois country. Every day

Indians and Northwoods-
men dried bear hides
this way.

the scouts went out ahead, but came back with nothing to report. Then, without warning while they were passing the Ottawa's narrowest point, arrows suddenly showered down on them from both banks. Painted faces appeared out of the dark foliage. War cries filled the air.

"Keep the canoes moving," shouted Radisson. "We'll outrun them."

The men bent low, their paddles flashing. The canoes shot down the river in a ragged line. From behind their beaverskin breastworks, some of the Hurons returned the fire.

The current and the furious paddling carried Radisson's flotilla through the ambush and out of danger. The boats glided along for several more miles. Then they pulled up to care for the wounded and to repair the canoes.

In those seven weeks they traveled 2,000 miles. At last they reached Montreal and paddled easily down the St. Lawrence to Quebec, then the capital of the North American fur trade.

It was late in August when the fleet reached port. A cannon salute from three French ships anchored in the bay greeted them. Quebec went wild with joy. Radisson and Groseilliers were the first traders to return to the settlement with any pelts since 1650. The two men were wined and dined by all the prominent citizens. Although received as a hero, young Radisson was far from satisfied. In his heart burned the fire of the true explorer—his was a spirit that always would be restless, always adventurous. It was his ambition to reach Hudson Bay, to pioneer the fur trade in that remote region. Perhaps, too, he would find the Northwest Passage, that fabled route to the riches of the Indies which fired the imagination of every explorer of that day. On his next expedition, he vowed he would succeed.

On the Trail of the Beaver

The use of fur for warm and protective clothing is spoken of in the Bible. In Europe, furs as trimming for garments were symbols of wealth and power. (This, of course, applied chiefly to men; it is only in recent times that furs have been worn to any extent by women.)

The most valued fur was the beaver. As far back as the twelfth century, trappers in Germany needed a special charter to hunt this animal, whose misfortune it was to possess a valuable fur. In the same century, Pope Lucius III, as a special favor, awarded a certain monastery the beaver rights within its area. Even before Columbus began his voyages, the animal had been hunted virtually to extinction in Europe.

The fur trade reached its height in the North American wilderness between the seventeenth and nineteenth centuries. The virgin forests and streams of America were teeming with wildlife. The Indians hunted the beaver, the marten, the otter, and other fur-bearing animals, but only in moderation and chiefly to keep themselves supplied with warm clothing.

It was the European who saw these animals, and the beaver in particular, as a commodity of unusual value. Soon France's sparsely populated colony in the New World, centered largely in what is now eastern Canada,

Beaver

Samuel de Champlain often fought with his Huron allies against the Iroquois.

came to depend on the fur trade for its commerce. As the demand for beaver hats and coats increased in Europe, the economy of New France flourished.

By the last decade of the sixteenth century, the fur trade had become so important and lucrative that France sought to do two things: to regulate the activities of the independent traders known as *coureurs de bois* ("runners of the woods"); and to protect them from the encroachments of others, particularly the English and the Dutch.

This was the situation that confronted the explorer Samuel Champlain. The rapid growth of the fur trade had attracted considerable attention in official circles in Paris. Champlain was an aristocratic-looking man with wavy black hair, a wide curling mustache, and a neatly trimmed goatee. As the royal geographer in the Court of the French King, Henry IV, he was regarded as a colonial expert. The French government sent Champlain across the Atlantic with an eye to controlling the trade and also to gain knowledge of the North American interior.

In 1603, the thirty-six-year-old explorer traveled the St. Lawrence on a voyage of reconnaissance and trade. He and his companions went beyond Hochelaga (the Indian name for what later was to become Montreal), proceeding as far as the Lachine rapids.

Champlain spoke to the Indians wherever and whenever he could. From what they told him, he was able to envision the existence of Hudson Bay seven years before it was discovered by Henry Hudson. Champlain also pointed out that in order for the French to explore America they would have to travel with the Indians and learn their ways—advice which future explorers were to take with great success and profit.

In 1608 he founded Quebec, with the intention of establishing it as a base for the French fur trade. Champlain also nurtured the dream of all early North American explorers —that he would find the Northwest Passage. From Quebec, he hoped to "penetrate inland as far as that half-mythical body of water known vaguely as the Western Sea, and thence at some future day to reach even to China."

Fur trappers followed many rivers deep into the wilderness.

Champlain drew this map of New France based on his exploration
of the St. Lawrence River and Indian descriptions of the land to
the west.

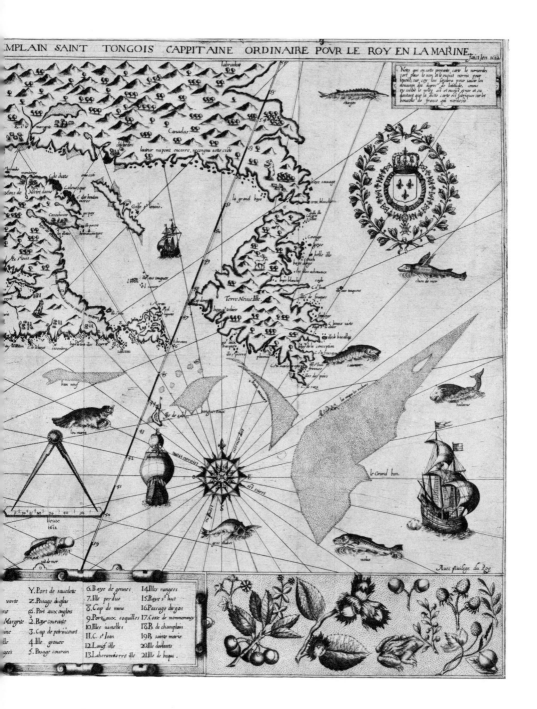

It was Champlain's task to organize the fur merchants and subject them to government control. Independent traders would henceforth require licenses. This was a system that would remain to plague young Pierre Radisson several decades later.

The chief object of the trade was a most remarkable animal—the beaver. Its pelt is one of the finest produced by nature. The beaver's thick fur covering consists of a rough, reddish-brown outer coat and a soft, silvery undercoat. It has a somewhat roundish head with small ears, a rather broad, scaly tail, and webbed hind feet. In length it is approximately thirty inches, not including the tail, and weighs from thirty to sixty pounds. The beaver is a marvelous swimmer, using its tail as a rudder.

Beavers live in a planned, orderly society. Using their claws, their tails and teeth with great skill, they build the "lodges" in which they live. These lodges are constructed of branches and twigs tightly plastered with mud, with two levels—one above water and one below. The underwater level contains their entrances and exits, for protection against enemies. The beaver usually builds his home in waterways whose shores are overgrown with shrubbery.

If the water is not deep enough to cover his doorways, the beaver constructs his famous dam out of tree trunks, branches, mud, and stones. His dam is remarkably strong, capable of resisting great water pressure. The beaver seldom leaves his home by day. When he does, he usually swims far enough under water so that he cannot be traced to his lodge.

Before the white man came, the Indian hunted beaver with bow and arrow. Then the almost universal method of catching beaver, a steel trap, was adopted. The trapper waded into the stream and planted his trap in three or four

Steel beaver trap.

A beaver colony as it appeared in the imagination of a European artist in 1715.

inches of water a little way from the bank. Next he fastened a five foot chain to a strong stick, which he drove into the stream bed. Over the trap he set a small twig on which a bait attractive to the beaver was placed. To reach the bait the beaver had to step on the trap, thus springing it.

Depending on the size of the animal, and the prevailing price of fur, a single skin would bring between four and ten dollars. It was the soft, downy inner fur, equipped with tiny, sharp barbs that made the hairs cling together, that was so ideal for making the felt of the so-called beaver hats.

"Regent" style beaver hat, 1825.

Since the Indians were nomads, they welcomed the traders' small iron cooking pots to replace their large wooden ones.

The Indians were accustomed to shooting or trapping the beaver when the coats were "prime"—in other words, at the coldest time of the year. They would dry the skins in the sun over a framework of branches, and rub the insides with the tallow of another animal to make them soft. Then they would sew six or eight skins together with animal sinews and wear them for a while as robes. By the time they were ready to offer them in trade, the guard hairs would have worn off, leaving only the soft underfur. Such pelts brought the highest prices.

At the height of the trade, North American fur companies were exporting as many as 200,000 skins annually. The beaver would almost certainly have become as scarce in the new world as it was in the old, had it not been for the abrupt change in European styles—the silk hat suddenly came into vogue in London in the 1830s. After that time the market in beaver skins sharply declined. But in Radisson's era, change in fashion was a long way off. The industrious little animal was to be the center of two centuries of drama and adventure before the first silk hats appeared on the heads of English gentlemen.

In the beginning, Indians came out of the woods and brought furs to the French, first to Quebec, then to Three Rivers, and finally to Montreal. The Huron hunting parties covered an area from the Sault River, connecting Lakes Superior and Michigan, extending northward several hundred miles to the southern end of Hudson Bay. Once a year their enormous canoe flotillas, laden with furs, came up the St. Lawrence. The Indians took back with them hatchets, knives, kettles, beads, and trinkets—the manufactured wares of the Old World.

The red men had always been eager to barter. Jacques Cartier, the great French explorer, wrote in 1534 of the natives in lower Canada, "They made frequent signs to us to come on shore, holding up to us some furs on sticks." After the trading was over, Cartier continued, the Indians "all went back naked without anything on them."

Jacques Cartier discovered Hochelaga, an Indian village he renamed Montreal.

Indians roamed the streets of 17th century Montreal, where they were welcome.

The Indians were dazzled by the goods the white man had to offer them. They had been using hatchets made of stone and needles fashioned from bone. Most important, their only kettles were large, hollowed-out tree trunks. In these they did their cooking, heating the water by dropping red-hot rocks into it. Suddenly "the men with beards," as the Indians called the French, appeared with kettles of iron and brass, things that would not burn or break. The smaller pots were especially welcome because they greatly increased the ability of the tribes, who were natural nomads, to move about. Later, the Europeans also traded to the Indians objects less benign—intoxicating liquors and "thundersticks." The thundersticks, with their loud noise and acrid smoke, were far more deadly than the bows and arrows of the redskins, and were to change the nature of their wars.

The Indians began to count on using goods from Europe in their daily lives. As they did so, they became less independent and more subservient. At first they had little of value to offer beyond their labor, and fresh fish and meat, nuts, or berries. Then they found that the bearded ones would give them things for fur—and fur they could find in abundance.

It was probably inevitable that after awhile the French would grow impatient waiting for the Indians to bring the furs to them, and would move westward themselves, drawn by the prospect of fortunes in fur. The government-controlled monopoly forbade them to do so, but it wasn't long before the more adventurous *coureurs de bois* began disappearing from the settlements and going out into Indian country.

The beaver lured them on. The animal, shunning his former habitat as people moved nearer his haunts, kept

Indians brought their game in to trade for the white man's goods.

Close friendships developed between the *coureurs de bois* and Indians.

retreating westward, pursued by the traders. The broad rivers were their high roads to the wilderness—the Ottawa, the Richelieu, the St. Lawrence. Traders crossed the Great Lakes to the land of the Crees and the Sioux. They traveled where no white man had ever set foot before. Upon their return, if they were laden with furs, they had no trouble finding merchants to participate in their illegal trade.

Today such great cities as Detroit and Chicago, Minneapolis and St. Paul, stand upon the sites where yesterday's explorers made camp. Superhighways stretch where they blazed trails through virgin forests with their moccasin-clad feet.

And so as a by-product of the fur trade, a continent was opened.

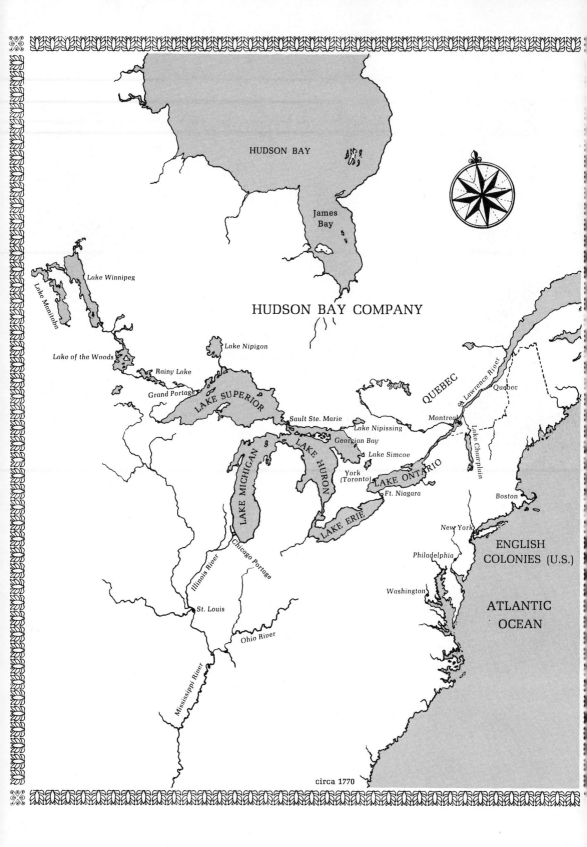

Escape from the Iroquois

Outstanding among these intrepid explorer-traders was Pierre Radisson. He was perhaps the most imaginative and resourceful, energetic and courageous of them all. He possessed unshakable faith in his ability to realize his most improbable dreams; and the American continent in the mid-seventeenth century was the dreamer's land. It was wide enough to accommodate the most restless spirit, abundant enough to feed the greatest ambitions.

The vision, energy and growth of today's America is epitomized in the story of Pierre Radisson. Born in Paris in 1635, by the time he was fifteen, he had already visited England, Italy, and Turkey as a cabin boy aboard French ships.

In 1651 Radisson came to Canada with his parents and his sister, Marguerite. The family settled at Three Rivers on the St. Lawrence, north of Montreal. Two years later, when he was seventeen, the reckless youth strayed from the settlement to go hunting with two other boys. They had been warned that the Iroquois, the mortal enemies of the French and their Huron allies, had been seen in the surrounding forests, but they went anyway.

In time Radisson's companions took fright and ran. Pierre continued on alone, nine miles into the cool, quiet forest. He was exultant and unafraid. He loved the wilderness; everything he saw filled him with a sense of excitement.

He had shot some geese and ducks and was on his way home. In fact he could see the church steeple at Three Rivers, when he stumbled upon the bodies of his two friends. Arrows bristled from their backs. They had been scalped.

Suddenly Radisson saw the forest around him moving. It was alive with Iroquois! They shot their arrows at him and the youth fired back. When they closed in on him he fought back valiantly, swinging and clubbing at them with the stock of his musket. The Iroquois were so impressed by his courage that they spared him.

The Indians took him to their camp on the Mohawk River in what is now central New York. Radisson's ability to hunt and fish and his indomitable spirit won the admiration of the Iroquois. The widow of a chief adopted him and he continued to live among them for more than a year.

Radisson's period of captivity with the Indians was to prove most valuable in the years ahead. He learned how to live off the land, how to read a trail, and, most useful of all, how to live and think like an Indian. He mastered the art of stripping the bark from a birch tree to make canoes. He learned how to use flexible cedar boughs for the sturdy crossribs, how to soak pine roots so they could be used for sewing the strips of birch-bark together.

The youth lived with the tribe for a year. Then he and an Algonquin prisoner killed three of their Iroquois captors in the woods and made their break.

They built a canoe and launched it on the Mohawk. Later they portaged to Lake Champlain and paddled north toward the St. Lawrence and Three Rivers. For fourteen days and nights they traveled through Iroquois country.

Rival traders race to an Indian camp to get first pick of the furs.

On the last lap of their journey, as they were crossing the St. Lawrence, within sight of home, a party of Iroquois in canoes came up behind and overtook them. The Iroquois opened fire; with the first volley they killed the Algonquin and sank the canoe.

Radisson was plucked from the water, trussed up and taken back to the Iroquois camp. Upon his return, he was tortured. The Indians drew out four of his fingernails. They held his thumb in a lighted pipe. They also "burned the soles of my feet and legs," he wrote, and one of his captors "run through my foot a sword red out of the fire." A little boy even tried to chew off one of his fingers.

Although his experience was scarcely a pleasant one, Radisson knew he was lucky to have escaped worse treatment. He lived to see other captives, both French and Huron, roasted alive.

Iroquois often tortured their captives. Here one prepares for a scalping.

If there was one thing the Indians respected above all others, it was stoic endurance of pain. Radisson's courage through two days of torture impressed the Iroquois. They welcomed him back into the tribe and soon made him a trusted warrior. Radisson wore the clothes of the Iroquois and covered his body with their paint. He went with them on raids against other tribes to the shores of Lake Ontario, beyond Niagara, and to the northwest.

Later, in 1653, he accompanied some Iroquois to the Dutch encampment at Fort Orange (now the site of Albany). The Dutch and the Iroquois had formed an alliance against the French and the Hurons. It was from the Dutch that the Iroquois received their firearms; therefore they were on friendly terms.

Radisson, dressed as an Iroquois warrior, fell into conversation with a Dutch soldier. Beneath the warpaint, the Dutchman recognized a white skin. The soldier offered to help him escape. Radisson refused, saying he was happy enough with his life among the tribe. But once back among the Iroquois, the youth began to feel homesick.

Pierre resolved to return to his people, to escape once and for all. He had to plan carefully, though. He knew well that a second escape would not be looked upon kindly by the Iroquois, in spite of his status as blood brother.

One day, after two weeks of plotting, he walked casually out of the village. Once in the woods, he began running, lightly, quietly. The powerful, tireless youth ran for a day and a night until he came to a cabin. It was inhabited by a Dutch family who agreed to conceal him. This was dangerous, for the Iroquois wanted Radisson back.

The Indians searched the forests and watched the river. They went to Fort Orange and inquired as to the whereabouts of the French youth. But the Dutch claimed to have no information about him.

When it was safe, Radisson sailed down the Hudson River to Manhattan Island. From there he boarded a ship and returned to France. But the Old World could not con-

Manhattan Island (New York) looked like this when Radisson sailed from there in 1628.

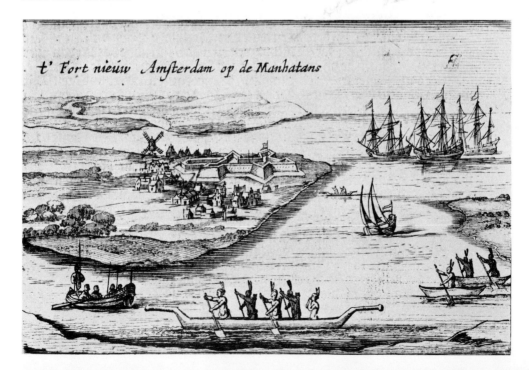

t' Fort nieuw Amsterdam op de Manhatans

Chipewyan Indian shoots the rapids in northern Minnesota.

tain his adventurous spirit for long. In the spring of 1654 he got passage on a French fishing boat headed for North America.

Upon reaching his home in Three Rivers, he found an addition to the household. His sister Marguerite, whose first husband had been killed by the Iroquois, had remarried. Radisson's new brother-in-law was Medard Chouart Groseilliers, although he was better known by his title, Sieur de Groseilliers. Their meeting was to have historic consequences.

Although Groseilliers was fourteen years Radisson's senior, they took to each other at once. In many ways they were temperamental opposites: Radisson was impetuous, quick-thinking, imaginative, excitable; Groseilliers was methodical, far-sighted, the cautious planner and good businessman. Yet these very differences, by their complementary nature, made possible their later exploits in opening up the interior of the continent.

They also had traits in common, such as a love of nature and adventure. Both were fascinated by new experiences, by solitude, by journeying into the unknown.

For weeks, sitting in their dooryard watching the ships glide by on the St. Lawrence, they must have swapped yarns—Radisson telling of his hair-raising adventures in trying to escape from the Iroquois, Groseilliers recounting his travels among the little-known tribes farther west.

Groseilliers' stories no doubt fired Radisson's vision, for in the fall of 1654, not many weeks after Pierre's return, the two Frenchmen launched their first westward expedition. Indians of the Huron and Ottawa tribes accompanied them. Up the St. Lawrence they went, then up the Ottawa. They portaged to Georgian Bay in Lake Huron. Then they canoed past the Mackinac straits through the rapids of the

Sault River, and into the Green Bay area of Lake Superior. There they spent the winter.

With the coming of spring in 1655, the Frenchmen and their Indian companions crossed Wisconsin. They were the first white men to reach that part of the Mississippi, coming upon it near the site of Prairie du Chien. They spent three weeks building canoes and then paddled down the river to Prairie Island.

There is still some dispute as to the location of the island on which the events described in Chapter I took place. But most historians now believe it to have been in the Mississippi in southern Minnesota.

Groseilliers remained in camp throughout the summer and autumn. He wanted to make sure that they grew enough corn for the journey home. Meanwhile, Radisson pushed on even farther. He spent four months going from river to river with a party of Indians, traveling southeast to the Illinois River.

As the leaves were beginning to turn, Radisson headed back to Prairie Island. He could feel the first chill breath of winter coming from the North. With his Indian allies he wandered about until winter set in, freezing the lakes and rivers, while bleak gray skies tumbled snow upon them.

Radisson was reluctant to return to camp. He had made a great find. All along the multitudinous lakes, streams, and rivers where he roamed, he saw beaver—and beaver in such numbers, of such size and richness of fur, as he had not known existed. Here, indeed, was a fortune for the taking.

The Frenchmen spent the winter on Prairie Island, content and excited over their prospects. With the coming of warm weather they would return to Quebec. And the beaver pelts they were bringing with them would be worth

An early imaginative drawing of the beaver.

a king's ransom. It was in the following spring that Radisson shamed the reluctant Indians and pressured them to make the return trip with him.

They reached Quebec as scheduled, and the entire settlement welcomed them as heroes. The sophisticated French, from the continent, and the Indians, fresh from the woods, mingled and made speeches, sat at banquet tables, danced and sang and intoned warriors' chants. Bonfires of celebration rose into the night, casting their eerie red glow out over the river.

Radisson gracefully accepted congratulations from everyone. But they meant nothing to him. Even in this moment of high triumph the intent, determined young explorer's thoughts were roving westward. This was merely the beginning. The greatest of his conquests were yet to come.

Trappers bringing their families and furs from the hunting grounds.

Into the Unknown

Radisson and Groseilliers grew restless under government restraint. Not only did they yearn to trade with the Indians, but also to explore.

The fur trade had remained essentially a monopoly since Champlain had organized the merchants and placed them under government control. Aside from some illegal trading by the *coureurs de bois*, all trade was centered at the settlements of Quebec, Montreal, and Three Rivers.

The merchants favored the system because it protected them from competition. The government maintained it because the Indians were compelled to bring their furs to the settlement, thus making them more and more dependent upon New France.

The monopoly placed great restraint upon the free spirits of New France—the *coureurs de bois*. These men could not be controlled indefinitely. More and more of them were leaving the settlements, traveling to the Indian country, and trading on their own.

Occasionally licenses were issued to the independent traders. But these licenses allowed the government to take what the traders considered to be an unfair share of the profits. Any independent traders who were caught without these licenses could be fined and taxed.

In the summer of 1659 Radisson and his brother-in-law

Ships such as these sailed from Montreal, their holds filled with furs
which Radisson and other trappers brought in from the wilderness.

were anxious to point their canoes westward once more. Montreal's new governor, the Vicomte d'Argenson, said he would grant them a license but only on condition that they take along two of his own men, with whom they were to divide the profits equally.

Radisson refused. "We made the governor a slight answer," he wrote, "and told him for our part we knew what we were, discoverers before governors."

They were forbidden to leave. Evidently, it did not occur to the governor that for the sake of his own greed, he was dealing New France's vital fur trade a serious blow.

Radisson and Groseilliers could not be stopped, however. In August of 1659, they stole away from the Three Rivers garrison and followed some of their Indian friends into the night.

For twenty-two days they paddled up the Ottawa River, plagued by attacks from the ever-harassing Iroquois. Finally they reached Georgian Bay and sailed the Northern Channel to the Sault.

Guided by a group of Ojibways, they navigated the Sault and paddled along the south shore of Lake Superior. This was the body of water that Cartier and Champlain believed would lead to the Pacific. It was autumn now, and from the lake Radisson, leading his silent flotilla, saw colors of unbelievable brilliance.

They passed Grand Island to Keweenaw Point, the northernmost tip of Michigan. Then they portaged, rather than make a prolonged circuit on the lake. On the shore of Chequamegon Bay, where the city of Ashland, Wisconsin, stands today, they constructed a log fortress. They stored their trading goods in the hastily improvised fort and made their way farther west, to the principal Huron village in the area. They reached their destination just as the first snows

Little Crow, Sioux warrior.

Hurons like these gave willing assistance to the French.

were filling the silent forests. It was here, in the vicinity of
Lac Courte Oreille, that they established their base camp
for the winter.

They dispatched runners to invite the neighboring tribes
—primarily the Sioux and the Cree—to come to a great
trading feast in the spring. The Frenchmen hoped, step by
step, to open the fur trade to more and more Indians over
an ever-widening area. By going out into the fur country
and establishing trading posts, they reasoned, they could
do more trading in less time. History was to prove this an
astute view. But it was one which made no sense just then
to the narrow-minded monopolists along the St. Lawrence.

Again Radisson was looking forward with eager antic-
ipation to the spring. But events that followed made it
doubtful whether he would live to see it.

The Indians with whom he was encamped did not have
enough corn to see them through the winter, when game
and fish were scarce. Hunting parties went out. A rendezvous with the Sioux was arranged for early January in the
vicinity of Knife Lake in present-day Kanabec County,
Minnesota.

Maize, or "Indian corn," kept trappers alive on long trips.

Radisson arrived at the rendezvous after a discouraging hunt. It was the dead of winter. There fell such "a quantity of snow and frost," he wrote, "and with such a thick mist, that all the snow stuck to the trees." He compared the darkness that it cast over the forest to an eclipse of the sun.

The two Frenchmen and the hundreds of Hurons huddled in their bark huts, shivering and gnawed by hunger. To complicate their problem, they were joined by a wandering band of 150 Ottawas. "The famine was great among many that had not provided beforehand," Radisson wrote. "It grows worse and worse daily."

The hunger was terrible that long, dark, cold winter in the Minnesota woods. Those who had enough strength left dug down through six feet of snow and then three feet of frozen ground to find roots. They ate their dogs and even their precious beaver skins. When these were gone, they ate wood. Radisson describes it:

"The greatest subsistance that we can have is of rind tree which grows like ivy about the trees; but to swallow it, we cut the stick some two feet long, tying it in bundles, and boil it, and when it boils one hour or two the skin comes off with ease, which we take and dry it in the smoke and then reduce it into powder between two grain-stones, and putting the kettle with the same water upon the fire, we make it a kind of broth, which nourished us. . . .

They did not think they would live out the winter. Many did not. Some 500 of the Indians perished.

The brutal season was over at last. Radisson and Groseilliers lived to keep their spring rendezvous with the Sioux. This was the tribe Radisson called "the nation of the beef," because of their stories of millions of buffalo that roamed across the plains to the west where most of the Sioux lived.

The Sioux had heard of the manufactured products—the

knives, hatchets, mirrors, bells, beads, combs, kettles—
Radisson had with him, and they were anxious to trade.
The Frenchmen welcomed them with great festivities.
Several days were passed in feasting, dancing, speech-
making, and the exchange of gifts, before getting down to
business.

The Sioux warriors impressed Radisson with their pomp
and splendor. As they arrived, carrying their long bows and
horn-tipped arrows, they made him think of "the entrance
that the Polanders did in Paris, saving that they had not so
many jewels and instead of them had so many feathers."

Fanciful stories inspired this drawing of a "crook-backed ox"
(buffalo).

Their faces were painted with many colors and "their hair turned up like a crown, and were cut very even, but rather so burned, for the fire was their scissors."

The Sioux were clothed in deerskin; each had the feathered skin of a crow (or perhaps a human scalp) hanging at his belt. Their shoes were made of buffalo hide. Some carried swords or knives that were over a foot long, and wooden clubs.

In spite of the amicable atmosphere, Radisson began to sense a certain suspicion on the part of his guests, a mounting tension. A muttering developed among the Sioux. One dissident group stood off by themselves, staring at him in sullen silence. Among them were a number whom Radisson judged to be powerful chiefs, arrayed as they were in magnificent war bonnets. They were unimpressed with the kettles that did not burn or wear out. They were unimpressed with the brightly colored blankets and the strings of beads and the mirrors in which they could see their own dour faces.

At this unexpected moment, Pierre Radisson had a flash of his characteristic resourcefulness. A campfire was blazing in preparation for the evening meal. When Radisson saw that the eyes of all the Sioux were upon him, he threw a handful of gunpowder into the flames. There was a sudden bang and a puff of smoke. The Sioux fell back, frightened. A moment later they were gazing at the young Frenchman with wonder and astonishment. Here was a man gifted with the powers of the supernatural—there could be no question of that. The dissident chiefs came forward and swore that they would look upon the French as masters of their lives.

"We were Caesars," Radisson wrote ironically, "being nobody to contradict us."

Radisson and Groseilliers then set out to cross Lake Superior. This was a dangerous trip. At that time of year the lake was filled with drifting ice floes which could smash the fragile canoes like eggshells. But the Frenchmen safely reached the other side, where they were warmly received by the Cree Indians. The Crees, it turned out, did the actual fur trapping in the region. They had been trading with the Huron and Ottawa tribes who in turn took the furs to the French.

The two explorers spent many months among the Crees. They experienced innumerable adventures, some of them nearly fatal.

At one point Radisson was suddenly felled by a mysterious paralysis. He was totally unable to move. Insisting that Groseilliers go ahead, he lay flat on his sled, while Indians pulled him to the next settlement. There his paralysis fled

Voyageurs had to use snowshoes to get about in the hard northern winters.

as mysteriously as it had come. Another time, his bark hut went up in flames while he slept. He barely escaped with his life.

Radisson was excited by something he kept hearing around the Cree campfires. That was a repeated reference to "the shining water that tastes of salt and is so wide you cannot see the far shore."

It must be the great inland ocean of which he had learned in other Indian legends. He was certain this body of water existed, even though others scoffed.

Northward and farther northward they pushed. Did they, on this trip, see Hudson Bay for themselves? Radisson's own journal is not clear on this point and it has been debated ever since. What Radisson did achieve on this journey was to open trading directly with the tribes who did the trapping.

Radisson and Groseilliers had taken the first step toward eliminating the middlemen—those Hurons and Ottawas who bought from the Crees and sold to the French. In the process they had also picked up a valuable piece of information. The Hurons and the Ottawas were expert canoeists; the Crees were not. If the French were to trade directly with the Crees they would have to become as expert at handling a canoe as the Hurons or the Ottawas.

Sometime in June, 1660, Radisson and Groseilliers embarked on their return journey to Quebec. Their flotilla was an impressive sight. With them went 700 Indians in more than a hundred canoes, laden down with some of the finest beaver skins ever trapped in North America. The two adventurers looked forward to a hero's welcome at both Quebec and Montreal. Their share of the cargo would make them wealthy. Now they would receive acclaim to match.

The Company of Gentlemen Adventurers

It was a clear, bright day in August, 1660, when Radisson and Groseilliers came up the St. Lawrence to Montreal. At their backs was a magnificent flotilla of pelt-filled canoes manned by hundreds of chanting Indians—"so great a number of boats" wrote Radisson in his journal, "that they did almost cover the whole river."

The sound of the chanting brought virtually all of the settlement's population running down to the riverside. They stood in awe as the swarm of birch-bark canoes, propelled by the strong, bare arms of Huron and Ottawa warriors, bore down upon the community.

A great cheer went up as they recognized Radisson himself, now twenty-five years old, paddling toward the shore.

In one way the welcome proved to be something quite different from what the young man had anticipated. No-one was on hand to extend him official greetings. Radisson and Groseilliers were summoned to report to the governor's quarters. There the angry official berated them for having gone into the fur trade illegally. Governor d'Argenson had neither forgotten nor forgiven Radisson's unauthorized departure.

"You disobeyed the regulations and traded without a license."

Louis XIV mistakenly ignored Groseilliers' information about North American riches.

"But surely we have earned your forgiveness," Radisson argued.

"You have earned only punishment," the governor replied.

The astounded brothers-in-law were taxed, fined, and otherwise penalized to the extent of more than 50 percent of their profits.

Radisson was outraged. "The governor," he wrote later, "seeing us come back with a considerable sum, and seeing that his time was expired and that he was to go away, made use of that excuse to do us wrong and enrich himself with the goods that we had so dearly bought . . . that he might the better maintain his coach and horses at Paris." Out of a cargo worth about $100,000, they could keep for themselves only $20,000. The rest was to go to the governor for penalties. Groseilliers was even imprisoned for a time.

The two woodsmen, burning with anger, decided that Groseilliers should go to Paris to present their case to Louis XIV. Groseilliers took ship for France; Radisson kept out of sight. For months, Groseilliers hung about the sprawling, luxurious palace at Versailles, a bearded, misplaced wanderer in buckskin.

In the pathways of the formal garden, in the antechambers of the glittering ballrooms, Groseilliers buttonholed anyone whom he thought he might intrigue with his tales of wilderness wealth. But the beribboned dandies of the court were too enmeshed in the complex affairs of Europe, too busy with their own schemes to pay much heed to the interloper. What they did hear of his tales was too far-fetched to believe, anyway.

Groseilliers spent long, frustrated weeks in France, but achieved nothing. Had the King or his courtiers only listened, the New World might have developed under the French, rather than the British. Embittered and disgusted, Groseilliers set sail for Canada. There he rejoined his brother-in-law once more on British soil, at Nova Scotia.

He found Radisson afire with a new dream—a sea route direct from the North Atlantic through the Hudson Straits into Hudson Bay, that vast inland ocean described to him by the Crees. Over such a route, ships loaded with knives, pots, and trinkets could proceed directly from Europe to remote trading posts on the shores of the bay.

Groseilliers looked like a barbarian amidst the luxury at Versailles.

Groseilliers started putting the wheels in motion. He approached some people from Boston who were in Nova Scotia on business. One of them, Captain Zechariah Gillam, merchant and ship-owner, agreed to finance the venture and take them in his own vessel. This was a man whom Radisson was to encounter later in what was to prove a critical situation.

The expedition set forth. They had reached the very mouth of the Hudson Strait, when snow began to fall. Captain Gillam, short-tempered and stubborn, put his foot down. With winter coming on, he would take his ship no farther into uncharted northern seas. He turned about and put back into Boston with the two explorers aboard.

Boston became a thriving North American port.

More exasperating delays followed. Because of the weather they had to wait nearly another year to resume their voyage. Then, backed by Boston merchants, they tried again. Once more they were forced to return without reaching the Bay. Worse—in their attempt they lost one of their two ships. As a result they became involved in a lawsuit which consumed most of what remained of their fortune.

For months they cooled their heels in Boston, trying unsuccessfully to raise money for another voyage. With their fortunes at their lowest ebb, word of their schemes reached the ears of the English King's commissioners. One of them, Sir George Cartaret, urged them to lay their plans before King Charles II. He himself would send them to England and arrange the audience with the King.

A few weeks later, early in 1665, the two Frenchmen sailed out of Boston Harbor. They were bound not for Hudson Bay, but for the English Court.

Their voyage could scarcely be called a peaceful one. The English and the Dutch were at war on the high seas. As their vessel neared the coast of Ireland, it was attacked by the Dutch and boarded. Sir George Carteret, Groseilliers, and Radisson all were taken prisoner and confined to the hold in irons. Eventually they were put ashore on the coast of Spain. It took them many weeks to make their way back to England.

While the men were en route, London was visited by the Black Death, the deadly plague which had been sweeping Europe and now had reached the British capital. Everyone who could had fled the city, including King Charles and his Court. They established themselves at Oxford, deep in the countryside.

Nevertheless arrangements were made for the audience with King Charles. The two travel-worn adventurers set out for Oxford in a fine coach drawn by four white horses.

Reaching the temporary court, Radisson and Groseillers, uncomfortable in their formal knee breeches, were ushered into a drawing room. There, seated in a deep chair of red velvet, and surrounded by sleek white hunting dogs, the King of England received them. Small, liquid, dark eyes looked at them curiously out of a dark-complexioned face. King Charles' long black hair fell to his shoulders. At his right sat his cousin, Prince Rupert, a dry, austere, stern-looking man, but one who listened attentively to everything Radisson said.

Radisson was so conscious of his gift of eloquence that he sometimes spoke of himself in letters as "your orator." He used that eloquence now to entrance his audience with

Charles II was intrigued by tales of North America.

his tales of the blood-thirsty Iroquois and the mighty Sioux, of the great salt water far to the north, and of his plan to sail into it straight from the Atlantic. He found his listeners spellbound by his stories of the unheard-of numbers of the beaver he had seen in those northern climes and the remarkable quality of their fur.

Standing before the King, Radisson appeared to be neither a self-seeking opportunist nor a deluded visionary. He was able to express all the love he felt for the wilderness beyond the frontiers in the new continent, as well as his faith in its future.

Whatever a man could desire was to be had there in abundance, he said, ". . . stags, fishes and all sorts of meat . . . corn enough . . . ." Of the Mississippi Valley: "I never saw a more incomparable country, for all I have been in

Prince Rupert arranged an expedition to Hudson Bay.

Italy. . . ." Of America's heartland, embracing the northern middle-western states and central Canada:

. . . the country was so pleasant, so beautiful and fruitful that it grieved me to see yet the world could not discover such enticing countries to live in. This I say because that the Europeans fight for a rock in the sea [Gibraltar] against one another, or for a sterile land and horrid country. Contrarywise those kingdoms [America] are so delicious and under so temperate a climate, plentiful of all things, the earth bringing forth its fruit twice a year, the people live long and lusty and wise in their way. What conquest would that be at little or no cost; what pleasure should millions of people have, instead that millions complain of misery and poverty.

King Charles, of French blood on his mother's side and having been an exile in his youth, had much in common with Radisson.

King Charles and Prince Rupert were impressed enough to take action. Through Rupert's efforts a group of English merchants who had his patronage were persuaded to equip an expedition to Hudson Bay for Radisson and Groseilliers. King Charles himself placed a ship, the *Eaglet*, at their disposal.

It had taken years, but the two Frenchmen were about to see their dream realized. They set sail from Gravesend at the western tip of England for North America in June, 1668. They embarked on separate ships, Radisson on the *Eaglet,* Groseilliers on the *Nonsuch.*

The two ships proceeded together as far as the north coast of Ireland, but there they encountered deadly storms. The *Eaglet* wallowed helplessly in heavy seas, on the point of foundering. To keep her from capsizing, it was necessary to chop away the mainmast. Radisson was forced back to England, where he spent months vainly trying to learn what had happened to his brother-in-law.

The *Nonsuch,* however, successfully navigated the North Atlantic, passed the southern tip of Greenland, and entered Hudson Strait south of Baffin Island. Then she sailed down through the cold, choppy waters of the Bay. In September, on the southeastern shore of James Bay, the southernmost extension of Hudson Bay, the English flag was raised—by a Frenchman.

Radisson, meantime, had outfitted another ship, and after many months delay, had set forth once more. This time the voyage was successful. In 1670 he reached the mouth of the Nelson River far up in the lowland area of the Bay, on the western shore. Eleven years had passed since the Cree Indians had described it to him during the long, famine-plagued winter at Lac Courte Oreille.

That same year the company received a charter along with an impressive title, "The Governor and Company of Adventurers of England Trading into Hudson's Bay." This was probably the most resounding name in the history of commerce.

In the name of King Charles II of England, the company received the sole right to trade in the area of all the Canadian rivers that emptied into Hudson Bay. In other words, all rivers that did not flow into the Atlantic, the Arctic, the St. Lawrence, or the Great Lakes, as well as all the land they drained—and all the beaver therein were part of the grant. The King had already given the new enterprise a boost by decreeing that henceforth all gentlemen's hats must be made of beaver.

Radisson and Groseilliers had brought the English to the northern and western margins of France's claim in the New World. The English flag had been raised. Their claim stretched nearly across the continent, a land mass embracing more than a million-and-a-half square miles. And they held a monopoly of the richest beaver country in the world.

It was the beginning of a hundred years' struggle for the continent between England and France. And where did Pierre Radisson find himself in this struggle? First on one side, then on the other, as he shifted his loyalties back and forth under the banners of the two contending nations.

Since it could take three months for a message to go from London to the lonely shores of the Bay, Radisson and Groseilliers were given considerable authority. Under its royal charter, the Hudson's Bay Company was empowered to build forts, enlist an army and navy, and otherwise rule itself with an unusual degree of independence. The two Frenchmen, reunited after months, were technically retained by the company as advisers. Being the only members of the company who could speak Indian languages, however, they undoubtedly increased their authority even more.

Before 1706, British flag was the Cross of St. George.

Groseilliers and Radisson set to work building Fort Charles on the shore of the Bay as the company's first trading center. But very soon Radisson grew restless. He left

Radisson sailed in the *Nonsuch* for Hudson Straits in 1668.

the building to his brother-in-law and set forth on an expedition which took him to the Moose and Albany rivers and to the mouth of the Nelson.

Radisson hoped to persuade the Indians to bring their beaver skins down the rivers to Fort Charles. This fort was to be the first in a series of trading centers built around the Bay. He insisted that posts be built at each of the three sites he visited. His eye for a favorable location was so uncanny that for two hundred years—in fact, until the coming of the steam trains—those posts remained crucial to the company's operations.

The English monopoly did not last long. In 1672, a mere two years after the charter was signed, the French began following the old canoe route down the St. Lawrence. They passed through the Sault and into Lake Superior. From that point they pushed northward into the territory south and southwest of Hudson Bay. There, since they were now in an area upriver from the trading posts, they were able to get their hands on quantities of the fur earmarked for the English.

The French entered what the English considered to be their private preserve. And they began to arrive regularly.

Radisson thought he knew how to stop the French raiding parties. He knew well the route the French had to take to reach the western fur country. He told his colleagues that if they would just build posts in certain key places, they would be able to prevent the French from coming in. Groseilliers supported him. But the English were thousands of miles from home, in a strange, vast wilderness, dealing with a people they did not know, whom they regarded as savages. Immediately the two French explorers were suspected of plotting to help their fellow Frenchmen.

Radisson, marching back and forth in front of a long table behind which Englishmen sat watching him, put forward his next idea. By expanding their sphere of activity to the northwest, he explained enthusiastically, they would more than make up for what the French were draining away in the south.

The English remained unconvinced.

"Listen to him," Groseilliers pleaded. "He knows well of what he speaks."

"I'm not tricking you," Radisson shouted. "There is no trick."

The tense and heated discussion went on for hours. At last the English grudgingly agreed to an exploratory voyage. But they continued to have misgivings about the idea.

One fine morning they all departed from Fort Charles, sailing north into the Bay.

During their absence an event took place that was to affect the future career of Radisson, the progress of the Hudson's Bay Company, and the whole of the fur trade in North America.

Inside a trading post.

An Incident at Hayes River

While the English were off taking inventory of the trading possibilities in the Northwest, a stranger, who had traveled overland, came upon Fort Charles and found it deserted.

The newcomer was a French-born Jesuit priest, Father Albanel. In the tradition of earlier explorers he claimed the post and the land around it in the name of France, and promptly hoisted the *fleur-de-lis*.

When the English returned and found the French flag flying over their fort, Charles Bayly, the company's first governor in America, flew into a rage. He accused Radisson and Groseilliers of having betrayed him. The bewildered Father Albanel produced English passports. Had he not, Bayly would have arrested him.

Bayly and the others were now convinced that the Frenchmen were disloyal to the company and the English. Bitter words and accusations were exchanged. The day came when Radisson could stand it no longer. He slammed his pipe down on the table and invited Bayly outside. In the clearing around Fort Charles the two men fought it out with bare fists until they could scarcely stand up, eyes blackened, faces battered, lips bleeding.

But the expenditure of energies did not reduce the tension and suspicion. Whenever Radisson and Groseilliers journeyed into the woods around the fort they found themselves being spied upon. They watched the English whispering among themselves, and took their meals alone. Their doors were meticulously locked at night. Even so, they seemed to sleep with one eye open.

Weary of playing cat-and-mouse, and fearing for their lives, the two Frenchmen slipped away from the fort one night. They followed the overland route back to the St. Lawrence.

Neither Radisson nor Groseilliers wanted to linger in French Canada, however. They booked passage for London to appeal their case. The English refused to rule in favor of two Frenchmen over their own people. The directors of the company, moreover, were at the moment delighted with the profits they were taking out of Hudson Bay. They saw no reason to upset the applecart.

Hoping to settle the dispute amicably, the directors asked Radisson to swear an oath of loyalty to the company. The proud *voyageur* viewed this demand as the crowning insult. He realized in what low esteem he was held by the company which owed its very existence to his vision, tenacity, and imagination.

Word of Radisson's wrath reached Colbert, Minister of Finance and favorite of the French King. Colbert dispatched a secret emissary to Radisson. He offered to restore citizenship to the two native-born Frenchmen. He also promised Radisson a purse of 400 gold Louis and a commission in the royal navy—all this if he would engage in the fur trade on behalf of Louis XIV. The timing of the French offer could not have been more perfect. Radisson and Groseilliers eagerly accepted.

Serving once more under the *fleur-de-lis*, Radisson returned to his beloved wilderness in 1682. The one-time boy explorer was now forty-seven years old. But his clarity of

The *fleur de lis*, insignia of the royal court of France.

Colbert, Louis XIV's minister, persuaded Radisson and Groseilliers to work once more for France.

vision, his enthusiasm, and his courage were undiminished. With a party of thirty, traveling in two vessels which were barely seaworthy, he crossed the Atlantic. He sailed through the Hudson Bay Straits and down the Bay to the mouth of the Hayes River. The Hayes, which fed into Hudson Bay from the southwest, could prove to be the key to the country Radisson had begged the English to open up to the fur trade.

Upon arriving, Groseilliers and the others began construction of a series of small log huts. They named the settlement Fort Bourbon in honor of the reigning house of France. Radisson remained there one day. The next day he left to go exploring.

No longer subject to the irksome restraints of the cautious English, Radisson once more gave full rein to his imagination and ambition. He traveled up the Hayes by canoe and then overland to Lake Winnipeg, southwest of the Bay. This exploration opened a route which for many years was to be a highway of the fur trade. He also made

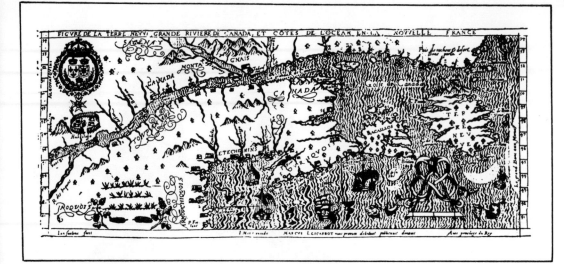

Map of St. Lawrence River, published in Paris, 1609.

friends with Indians who inhabited this vast tract of land. He persuaded a number of them to trade with the French at Fort Bourbon.

As he approached the fort, Radisson had reason to be pleased by his accomplishment. His pleasure was to prove short-lived, however. Trouble was waiting for him.

On the day he returned to Fort Bourbon he heard a cannon booming at the mouth of the river. As the echoes died away mournfully over the vast, silent land, Radisson listened and wondered what the sound meant.

As much as he resisted the thought, he could not escape the conviction that these were the guns of a Hudson's Bay Company ship. Had the company already discovered his hastily hammered-together fort and its meager garrison? This vessel from the rival company could, if it chose, blow the puny place to pieces. It could sink the two leaky vessels in which his party had come, and force his men to scatter into the wilderness.

Radisson, taking three men with him, crossed the tongue of land that lay between the Hayes and Nelson Rivers. When they reached the Nelson, the direction from which he had heard the firing, they saw a ship moored near an island off the northern banks of the river. To Radisson's amazement, it was not a ship from Hudson's Bay Company. It was *The Bachelor's Delight*, a pirate ship.

The Bachelor's Delight was out of New England and was under the command of one Ben Gillam. Gillam cruised along Hudson Bay in areas adjacent to those trapped by the English and the French. His business was poaching (illegal trapping)—a most serious offense in the eyes of both the English and the French.

Gillam was friendly enough when Radisson hailed him, and invited him aboard. But Radisson was suspicious. Only when two of Gillam's men agreed to wait on shore with the three Frenchmen did Radisson board *The Bachelor's Delight*.

Gillam had more men than Radisson and he had superior firepower. Radisson's only recourse was a bluff. He declared that he had already claimed the entire area for France and that he had under his command two large ships, a full contingent of well-armed men, a sturdy fort. He also claimed that he was expecting more ships from France at any moment.

At any cost, he had to keep Gillam away from Fort Bourbon. Otherwise the pirate would see Radisson's true position. In the most helpful and confidential tone, the Frenchman therefore suggested that Gillam keep his men confined to the island. If Gillam were to let them go ashore, he said, they were likely to be attacked by the French who were stationed all along the river banks.

Radisson's fabrications were convincing. Gillam was impressed. He poured two tots of brandy and proposed that they all live together in peace. They clicked glasses and drank. Then Radisson took his leave.

So far so good. He had bluffed Gillam with great success. But as he headed back to Fort Bourbon he couldn't help wondering how much longer he would be able to maintain his deception. Was there some way he could capture *The Bachelor's Delight* and her crew? By doing so he would remove this threat to Fort Bourbon.

But even as he mulled over this possibility, Radisson spotted a large ship coming up the Nelson under full sail. The vessel was the *Prince Rupert*. It belonged to the Hudson's Bay Company! Ironically, it was coming to establish a post in the same area which Radisson had once urged the company to exploit.

If the ship maintained its present course it would reach Gillam and learn of the presence of Fort Bourbon. Then, Radisson was certain, the pirates would conclude an alliance with the English against the French.

Instead of abandoning the weak fort, as he might have done, once more Radisson decided to brazen it out. He landed at once and built a fire on the shore. Seeing a bonfire in that deserted area, he realized, would attract the attention of those aboard ship. He knew they would investigate.

The ruse worked. The Hudson's Bay ship dropped anchor. A boat was lowered and it started for the shore.

Just as the small boat was being beached, Radisson stepped out of the bushes. He covered the landing party with his musket. At a signal, three other Frenchmen with drawn guns also emerged from the brush. In the dim twilight, by the gruff exchange of orders, they gave the impression that each was commanding a detachment of men.

The leader of the party introduced himself as John Bridgar, new governor of a fort the Hudson's Bay Company planned to build. A shout went up from his companion, the captain of the ship. He had recognized Radisson, who at the same time recognized him. He was Captain

Zechariah Gillam out of Boston, the man who had taken Radisson and Groseilliers on their first attempt to reach Hudson Bay. He was also the father of the pirate, Ben Gillam, but he did not know that his son was anchored only a few leagues away.

Radisson informed the astonished Englishmen that the French had taken possession of the territory. Although Bridgar protested friendliness, Radisson gave him the same story he had spun to young Gillam, repeating his description of a strong fort and a well-armed garrison. He warned against allowing any of the *Prince Rupert's* crew to wander in the forests. He also advised against the ship's proceeding farther up the river.

The Englishmen, convinced of Radisson's strength, invited him to dinner aboard the *Prince Rupert*. The impatient guest stuffed himself with venison and corn and bread, washed down with great drafts of brandy. Then he abruptly took his leave and hurried back to Fort Bourbon to inform Groseilliers of the situation.

Radisson and Groseilliers both preferred life in the wilderness.

Indians trapped in winter when fur was prime. Here they spear muskrats.

Radisson continued to play his tricky and most dangerous game. He returned to the Nelson River and found the English building a fort on the shore, with the *Prince Rupert* aground in the mud. He presented Captain Gillam with fresh game and generally ingratiated himself with the English, who probably thought him a very fine and generous fellow.

He then went on to visit the younger Gillam. The pirate captain had by now erected a solid fort, on which he had mounted cannon. He obviously felt secure in his position, for he began voicing some doubt about Radisson's strength at Fort Bourbon.

Again Radisson's wily mind went to work. He informed the younger Gillam that his father was anchored some miles up river. Because the Hudson's Bay Company people would not welcome poachers, Radisson offered to disguise young Gillam as a Frenchman and bring him to see his father.

Radisson's true intentions were less selfless and more subtle. He reasoned that if the senior Gillam knew that his son was nearby with a pirate ship he would prevent Bridgar's hearing about it. Thus any possible alliance between Englishmen and pirates against the French would founder. So Radisson carefully arranged for father and son to meet aboard the *Prince Rupert*. No one suspected the younger Gillam's true identity.

But Radisson's troubles were piling up. The elder Gillam, as well as the younger, had grown suspicious of the Frenchman. By coincidence, both factions dispatched spies at the same time to determine the true strength of Radisson's garrison. The crafty, forest-wise Frenchman captured them all.

By this time the cold, subarctic winter had set in. Radisson had warned Captain Gillam that the anchorage of the *Prince Rupert* was unsafe. But the captain, with some displeasure, refused to heed Radisson's advice. "He said he knew better what to do than I could tell him," Radisson said.

Gradually the river froze and the ice closed around the *Prince Rupert* in an ever-tightening vise. In the words of Radisson's journal, the ship "was staved to pieces, and the captain, lieutenant, and four seamen drowned." Four other Hudson's Bay men got safely away from the ship, only to die on shore. The elder Gillam was dead. The *Prince Rupert* was gone and its crew was either dead or demoralized. As a threat to the French, Governor Bridgar had been neutralized.

But Radisson still had Ben Gillam to deal with. Having brought his fort up to substantial strength, he was anxious to see Radisson's garrison. The cunning Radisson, who seems to have had no end of tricks up his sleeve, invited

Gillam and his men to visit Fort Bourbon. The poacher and his crew accepted eagerly. While they were en route, Radisson and his men slipped around a back way and took possession of Gillam's superior outpost, which was meagerly defended.

Gillam and his men were baffled to discover Radisson's fort deserted. They returned at once to their own fort, and found a surprise awaiting them. Radisson's men, heavily armed, surrounded them. Gillam and his men were prisoners in their own fort. Radisson then, by another ruse, also lured the remnant of the Hudson's Bay contingent to Gillam's fort. He took them prisoner as well.

Thus Radisson had successfully outwitted and outmaneuvered two sets of opponents, both superior to him in numbers and firepower. He had done it without shedding a drop of blood.

Indians made large, sturdy canoes from sheets of birch bark.

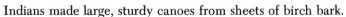

When the Indians came down the Hayes River the next spring with their furs, the French got all the pelts. The more adventurous French had set their pattern of outdoing the English in the fur trade—a pattern that would persist for many years.

The trading concluded, Radisson set sail for Quebec, taking with him his prisoners and his beaver skins. For a second time Radisson and Groseilliers, returning in triumph and expecting acclaim, were deeply disappointed. For reasons that were not explained, the Governor of New France immediately ordered the English and American prisoners released. He directed that Ben Gillam's ship be returned to him. He informed Radisson and Groseilliers that they were to take a ship at once for France, where they would be given a chance to defend their actions at Hudson Bay.

Radisson, standing before the governor as the latter barked out his intentions, listened in stark amazement.

"Why is this being done?" he demanded.

"It is not your place to question the decisions of your superiors," the governor replied.

"But everything we did was in the name of France," Radisson declared.

"You will not question your superiors," the governor repeated, his voice harsh.

"My superiors," Radisson said coldly, "did not sail with us on the icy waters of the Bay, nor did they go hungry with us in the wilderness."

"Nevertheless," the governor observed with finality, "you will return to France."

A new blow awaited the explorers when they arrived in Paris. Colbert, their mentor, was to plead their case. Upon first inquiry they heard the news: Colbert was dead.

Wherever they turned, they found themselves treated as little better than criminals. Strangely enough, their chief accuser was not a Frenchman, but the English ambassador, Lord Preston. He charged them in Louis' court of having "cruelly abused the English, robbed, stolen, and burned their habitation." Preston "demanded satisfaction, and that exemplary punishment might be inflicted on the offenders."

The whole case was so ridiculous that Radisson naturally expected to be found innocent. But what he did not know was that the two Kings, Louis and Charles, had signed a secret treaty. Thus, eager though the former was to possess the fur-rich, territory of North America, he would not do anything to offend Charles.

Much to his surprise, Radisson was ordered by the French Department of Marine to go to London and then back to the Nelson River on Hudson Bay. There he was to turn over the fort and everything in it to the English. Radisson found the order particularly irksome, for he alone knew that locked up within the fort were 12,000 skins, mostly beaver—a small fortune.

The humiliation, wounded pride, and disappointment, weighed heavily upon Radisson. He had worked long and hard, and had endured much in exploring the North American wilderness. His motive had not been simply personal gain; he also believed firmly in the destiny of America. He loved its natural beauties, its rivers, and its lakes. If he was not to be given riches and power, then Radisson believed he was due at least recognition and acknowledgment. He received nothing.

Feeling thus betrayed, it was inevitable that Radisson should switch sides once more and seek to return to the service of the English and the Hudson's Bay Company.

General store where Indians traded furs for guns.

King Charles was delighted to have him back. He instructed the company, Radisson wrote, "to have care of my interests and to remember my services."

But the way Radisson was treated hardly lived up to his expectations. Upon returning to his beloved Northwest in 1685, he was forced to sign a bond for 2,000 pounds to insure his fidelity to the company. Radisson worked hard and kept faith with his employers, but his fortunes continued to decline. Groseilliers had become inactive and retired before he died. When the French poaching raids cut into company profits, Radisson's pay was reduced. In 1692, he was approached by fellow traders who wanted him to join in a plot to cheat the company. Radisson indignantly refused. He was beaten and thrown into prison for his pains. For the rest of his life he was given a pension that represented only the tiniest fraction of the riches he had earned for others. Once, even that pension was taken from him, but he sued for its recovery and won.

Pierre Esprit Radisson died in London in 1710 at the age of seventy-five. The youth who had run with the Iroquois, who had pioneered the opening of the northern fur trade, who had fought the wilderness and the Indians, and who had ridden the great rivers and lakes of the North, was an almost forgotten figure. But Radisson had left as his monument the well-traveled trails over which the fur trade would flow and the great Hudson's Bay Company, through which that trade would flourish.

The crest of the Hudson Bay Company, chartered as "gentlemen adventurers."

Land of the Shining Mountains

In defiance of the secret treaty between the Kings Louis and Charles, the French continued to consolidate their position in the fur trade. True, the English were by now well-established on Hudson Bay. But that did not prevent the French from making greater and greater inroads. The courtiers—members of Louis' Court—could not overlook the great profits to be made.

In 1685 two ships under the command of Captain La Martiniere sailed into Hudson Bay. They were under orders to get all the fur they could, by all possible means.

It was an elaborately conceived scheme. The French sent one Jean Pére, a tough-minded half-breed, with two companions overland from Montreal to Fort Albany on the shores of the Bay. They were to pretend they were travelers. But Pére's real mission was to cooperate with La Martiniere's ships in the capture of the fort.

La Martiniere encountered several Hudson's Bay vessels in the ice-filled waters at the west end of the Strait. The smaller company ships turned and tried to get away. Some succeeded. But the heavy guns of La Martiniere's ships damaged one, and it was captured. Fourteen of the crew were killed.

The French did not go ahead and complete the plan, but instead repaired at once to Quebec, leaving Pére and his companions stranded.

News of the encounter in the Strait quickly spread. Pére was arrested and thrown into the dungeon at Fort Albany, where he was put in irons. He was later sent to England. His two companions were left on Charlton Island to the south, in James Bay. The English were convinced that the island—twenty miles from the mainland—was a place from which no one could escape.

But the English underestimated the resourcefulness of the two Frenchmen. The latter put together a makeshift boat and got across to the shore, then proceeded to make their way 1,000 miles overland to Montreal.

Tidings of Pére's imprisonment stirred New France as nothing else had done for a long time. It hardened the French resolve to drive the English from the North. Just at this time, in 1685, King Charles II suddenly died. The secret treaty between England and France was automatically dissolved.

For the French, the treatment accorded Pére became an excuse to attack the English. But what they were really after was control of the increasingly lucrative fur trade. The determined French sought to open up the interior of the United States and Canada to the trade. The English "Gentlemen Adventurers," on the other hand, reasoned that if they paid the Indians well and treated them fairly, they would bring their furs into the trading posts. The French, rather than the English, were profiting from the lessons taught by Radisson.

The cry to avenge Pére resulted in a military operation that took everyone by surprise. The Chevalier de Troyes, with one hundred men—thirty-three French and sixty-seven Indians—marched on snowshoes overland from Montreal to Lake Abitibi. There the men built canoes in which they ran the rapids. They then made their way by river to Hudson Bay.

Moose factory, important trading post of the Hudson's Bay Company, in 1850.

A mere hundred men, 1,000 miles out in the wilderness, proceeded to take the English post at Moose Factory. Then the contingent sailed eastward across the southern part of James Bay and took Fort Rupert, as well as the company ship they found riding at anchor.

With the captured ship they set out to seize Fort Albany, lying to the northeast. Forewarned by some Indians, the English and their civilian employees became alarmed. The employees demanded a pay raise before they would fight, and when they heard the French were bringing cannon with them they hid in the cellars of the fort.

The French laid siege to the fort for two days. Then the English surrendered. They marched out with bands playing and flags waving, were given their freedom, and marched away. When winter came thirty of them, trying to make their way back to civilization, starved to death in the wilderness.

One of the leaders of this military coup had been the vigorous Pierre Le Moyne d'Iberville, who was to make his name as a great hero of New France.

French warships won at Hayes River.

D'Iberville returned to Hudson Bay, where he continued to harass the company's outposts. He captured fort after fort until the Hudson's Bay Company, which by the King's charter had been granted so huge a piece of Canada, had remaining in its whole vast territory only one post.

By 1697 France and England were at war. In that year d'Iberville made history on the waters of the Hayes River. Five Hudson's Bay Company ships, heavily manned and armed, caught up with his ship, the *Pelican*. Sails dotted the horizon on every side. All avenues of escape were cut off. D'Iberville sailed out and attacked.

There was a deafening exchange of gunfire, with the echoes rolling back and forth across the waters. The English man-of-war *Hampshire* burst into flames and sank, taking with her fifty-two guns and all hands—estimated to be as many as 250 men.

A second English ship ran up the white flag; the others fled before d'Iberville could bring them under his guns. A gale blew up over the Bay, churning the waters to a froth. The captured vessel was wrecked; d'Iberville's own ship, the *Pelican*, was driven ashore and abandoned. D'Iberville and his men were eventually rescued by the remainder of his squadron.

A treaty signed between Louis XIV and England at Byswick ended the war. The treaty stipulated that each side should be permitted to hold what it already had in Hudson Bay. Only Fort Albany was left in the hands of the Hudson's Bay Company, while the richest post on the Bay, York Factory, along with other choice posts, fell to the French.

Each season for the next sixteen years both French and English ships entered the Bay. But the French reaped by far the richer harvest of beaver skins.

The Hudson's Bay Company fell upon lean years. Profits which in one year had reached 50 percent, now grew extremely slim. Some years there were none at all. Debts piled up.

On the continent of Europe, England and France had been on opposite sides in a long series of wars. Then, in 1713, by the treaty of Utrecht, these wars ended. The treaty had its repercussions in the New World. By its terms, the French were forced to cede large areas of North America. One of these areas was the vast territory surrounding Hudson Bay.

Unexpectedly, the English found themselves in control of lands where the fur trade potential was rich. This was no longer an unknown region. They had gotten back their forts, from which they could now operate. They still believed that if the Indians knew that they paid fair prices for furs they could sit in their trading posts and wait for the fur-laden Indians to come to them.

York factory was a rich fur trading post on Hudson Bay.

Such initiative as did appear was usually demonstrated by individuals who acted without specific instructions from the company. One of these individuals was a young man named Henry Kelsey, who had gone to work for the company when he was fourteen.

Early company records show Kelsey as something of a problem, often in trouble for breaking rules or even climbing the fort pickets at night and running away. But once his coltish spirits were given an outlet, he began to function effectively for the company. He had served for a time with Radisson at Fort Nelson. It may have been from Radisson that he got his love for the wilderness and for exploring.

In any event, his dynamic qualities were so outstanding that it is not surprising that he came quickly to the attention of his superiors.

In 1689 the company directed that Governor Geyer "send the boy Henry Kelsey to Churchill River because we are informed he is a very active lad, delighting much in Indian company, being never better pleased than when he is traveling amongst them."

Kelsey was only nineteen when, in that same year, he made his first journey to the far North. The trip was to be a landmark in the annals of exploration of that part of the world.

He started out with a young Cree Indian as his only companion. First they boarded a sloop that sailed through uncharted waters along the west coast of the Bay, progressing above the Churchill River. As they reached the northern waters, they encountered more and more ice, which made the going slow. Kelsey became impatient. He asked to be set ashore so that he could continue his travels on

The Cree tribe, plains Indians, lived in wigwams like this one.

Crees moved from place to place to find new hunting grounds.

foot. Thus he and his young Indian friend began an overland journey into the cold northern Bay country—an area never before visited by a white man.

Indeed, a hundred years were to pass before another white man would enter this bleak country. Kelsey found himself in a land where blizzards raged in August. He had to depend on shooting a stray caribou or musk ox for his food.

The boys were also invading a territory inhabited by tribes of Indians who might prove friendly—or who might not.

By the time they had penetrated 200 miles inland from the shores of the Bay, the young Cree became apprehensive about possible dangers ahead and refused to go any farther. Reluctantly, Kelsey returned to the Fort. He had not opened up any new sources of trade but he had become the first employee of the company to make an extensive journey without benefit of canoe.

In the summer of 1690, some Assiniboin Indians came east to Fort Nelson from their home in unknown wilderness country on their annual trading trip. Governor Geyer assigned Kelsey to take another trip inland, returning with the Assiniboins.

The purpose of the trip was to "call, encourage and invite the remoter Indians to a trade with us." Kelsey left York Factory in June, 1690. He followed Radisson's route up the Hayes River, thence over an old Indian canoe route from Oxford Lake to Lake Winnipeg. From there he journeyed up the Saskatchewan River into Cedar Lake. By July he had established a base of operations in the wilderness somewhere between Cedar Lake and Lake Winnipegosis, in what is now central Manitoba.

Kelsey was the first to make contact with the northern plains Indians. He tried to mediate in the wars between these tribes and those living closer to the Bay, but had only mixed success.

In the fall of 1690 Kelsey, accompanying an Indian hunting party southwest from Saskatchewan, suddenly came out onto the Canadian plains. Here was an expanse of prairie almost fifty miles wide, affording "nothing but beast and grass," the astounded explorer wrote.

Kelsey had by now gone farther west than any other white man. He discovered a land fabulously rich in beaver pelts. Not only was he the first Englishman to sight a buffalo and a grizzly bear, but he also met Indians who described to him "a great wall of mountains" (the Rockies) hitherto unknown to the European explorers.

Kelsey lived with the plains Indians for two years. He wore their leather garments; he hunted with them across the great prairie and in the forests. Only with some reluctance did he at last return to civilization. He brought "a good fleet of Indians" to York Factory with him to trade.

A tremendous opportunity was thus presented. But the "Gentlemen Adventurers" did nothing then to follow through on Kelsey's magnificent discoveries.

Henry Kelsey's remarkable feat of travel and discovery, therefore, yielded little tangible return. The youth remained with the company in various capacities, rising to Governor in 1718. He died sometime around 1730.

After the Utrecht Treaty of 1713, which gave the Bay area to the Hudson's Bay Company, the French set about developing their foothold in the Great Lakes region, especially around Lake Superior. Although they made some substantial inroads into the English trade, an entire season passed before they made the canoe journey from Montreal and back.

In 1728 another great French pathfinder, in the tradition of Champlain and Radisson, emerged upon the scene. He was Pierre Gaultier de Varrennes, Sieur de La Vérendrye. He was Canadian-born, but was a veteran of the European wars.

Encountering a bear was frightening, as this stylized picture shows.

Assinaboin Indians told Verendrye of the land of "shining mountains."

La Vérendrye was in charge of the French post on Lake Nipigon, north of Lake Superior. Hearing from Indians of the expanse of land to the west, he decided to explore it. It was Vérendrye's plan to establish trading posts in this western region. By doing so he hoped to prevent the Crees and the Assiniboins, coming out of the fur-rich lake regions west of the Bay, from going down the Hayes or Albany Rivers to the Hudson's Bay Company.

Vérendrye also believed that he might yet find the fabled Western Sea—in other words, the Northwest Passage. The Indians who sat night after night by his roaring fire and drank his brandy, drew maps on pieces of bark, directing him to the vast land to the west, describing a rich land of plains and lakes and "shining" mountains.

When La Vérendrye reported back to the King, he was ordered to return and claim as much land as possible for France. In contrast to the treatment accorded Radisson, he was to keep for himself whatever profits he might make out of the fur trade along the way.

This resolute explorer, the last of the great French pathfinders in North America, began his journey in 1731. He and his sons pioneered a route through the maze of waterways to Rainy Lake on the northern edge of what is now Minnesota, establishing the trade route that was to be known as Grand Portage. By 1733 he had reached Lake Winnipeg.

Vérendrye built Fort St. Pierre at the outlet of Rainy Lake. He also built Fort St. Charles at Lake of the Woods and Fort Maurepas near Lake Winnipeg. Fort Maurepas was particularly important, for it was situated squarely athwart one of the main Indian routes to Hudson Bay, thus effectively cutting off much of the English trade.

The French now held a network of forts across the very heart of the continent's richest fur area. It was the same land that had been given to the Hudson's Bay Company by charter.

Then the British company stirred itself into action. In 1754 a young man named Anthony Henday was dispatched inland. His mission: to dissuade the Indians from trading with the French. Henday left York Factory in June, 1754. With some Assiniboin companions, he followed the route taken up the Hayes River by Radisson and later by Kelsey—the route which later was to become a primary artery of the fur trade.

Like all previous travelers, Henday learned to live and eat—and occasionally to starve—like an Indian. He wore the Indians' leather garments and lived in their teepees.

After four weeks of travel, Henday and his party had passed Lake Winnipeg. He proceeded by canoe through the swamp land of the Nelson and the lower Saskatchewan. Eventually he visited one of the French trading posts at Basquia, now known as The Pas, a Canadian town still active in the fur trade.

At Basquia the French sought to detain Henday. His Assiniboin companions moved in and threatened to put the fort to the torch and all the French to the knife. The French smiled politely and allowed Henday to go on his way.

Henday continued his travels through the summer and fall of 1754. Traveling far enough to emerge on the great plains, in buffalo country, he became the first Englishman to see members of the mighty Blackfeet tribe. Unlike the eastern tribes, these Indians rode horses.

Wherever he went Henday learned, to his distress, that the Indians preferred trading with the French, whose outposts were much nearer than those of the English. Making the long journey to and from Hudson Bay, they said, was for them to risk starvation.

He spent the winter on the plains between Calgary and Edmonton, in what is now Alberta, almost within sight of the Rockies. He managed to present his company's case convincingly, and in the spring he started his return journey to York Factory accompanied by sixty canoes loaded down with pelts.

All went well until Henday arrived at a French post above Basquia. He and his party were given a royal welcome. Then, in spite of Henday's protests, the French plied his Indians with brandy. Remaining sober themselves, they then started a vigorous barter. Before Henday could get his flotilla moving again all of the finest furs had gone to the French.

When Henday declared he had seen Indians (Blackfeet) on horseback, nobody believed him.

Henday returned to York factory leading a 60-canoe flotilla.

Henday returned to York Factory. What he had seen and heard, what the French were up to, nobody would believe. The total disbelief was based upon one singular detail: he had seen Indians on horseback. Anthony Henday was mocked and ridiculed. He became so angry that he left the service of Hudson's Bay Company. And the English remained sitting in their forts on the Bay while the French continued to intercept the trade and drain the blood from the company.

In an effort to diversify their interests, the company sent an expedition to the northern reaches of the Bay in November, 1769. The purpose was twofold: to discover the copper mines, which they had heard about from the Indians, and to try once more to find the fabled Northwest Passage to the Orient.

In command of this expedition was a seaman named Samuel Hearne who, although only twenty-four years old, was a veteran, having joined the navy when he was eleven. He later resigned to enter the service of the Hudson's Bay Company.

Chipewyan Indian.

For many years the Chipewyans, Indians from the far north, who had come to the mouth of the Churchill River to trade, had displayed copper ornaments and utensils. So, on November 6, 1769, young Hearne, accompanied by several white men and a band of Indians, set out on the "Coppermine Expedition."

By November 29, Hearne was already in trouble. Some of the Indians deserted, taking the bulk of his supplies with them. Weak with hunger, the demoralized Hearne had to turn back. He arrived at Fort Churchill on December 11, to his "own great mortification."

But the young seaman was determined to carry out his mission. On February 23, 1770, in the midst of the terrible winter, Hearne set out a second time, accompanied again by Chipewyan Indians.

From the first, the expedition suffered from cold and hunger. They had to cross barren ground that was covered only by occasional patches of moss which were barely enough to feed the deer. Soon starvation was upon them.

"Sometimes we had too much, seldom just enough, frequently too little, and often none at all," Hearne wrote. "We have fasted many times two whole days and nights, twice upwards of three days; and once near seven days, during which time we tasted not a mouthful of anything, except a few cranberries, water, scraps of old leather, and burnt bones."

The men had no firewood. When they did bring down game they had to eat the meat raw. Nevertheless, in spite of many delays and hardships, Hearne crossed the Kazan River along the western rim of Yath-Kyed Lake, finally making a circuit around Dubawnt Lake, a body of water that never lost its covering of ice. This long trek was made through unbroken expanses of barren, desolate ground.

Hearne, an ex-seaman, calculated his position out of habit by nautical instruments. On August 11, a strong wind smashed Hearne's sextant beyond repair. Without this instrument Hearne was unable to determine where he was, so he started back to Fort Churchill. He had failed for a second time in his quest for the Coppermine River.

The return trip was another ordeal. Deserted by his Indian companions, Hearne trudged all alone across the

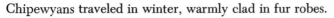

Chipewyans traveled in winter, warmly clad in fur robes.

empty, wind-blown northern lands. He was cold and he was hungry. Gradually he became weaker. He was suffering severely from starvation and exposure when a Chipewyan chief named Matonabbee encountered him.

Matonabbee was a "Northern Indian," a man of great skills and intelligence. He had lived at Fort Churchill where he had been useful to the company in bringing tribes to trade. With his assistance, Hearne made it back to Fort Churchill.

Hearne remained resolute, and on December 7, 1770, he set out a third time in search of the Coppermine River. This time Matonabbee as well as other Chipewyans accompanied him. They traveled along the edge of the forest instead of striking immediately into the barren interior. There, at least, they did not lack fuel, and they also received some protection from the biting winds.

Due to Matonabbee's foresight, they carried wood for tentpoles and skins for tents as well as moccasins, winter clothing, and plenty of birch-bark for making canoes. They ate caribou they killed along the way.

The party reached the Coppermine River in July and soon crossed into the Arctic Circle. Here his Indian companions paused and, ignoring Hearne's pleading, massacred a band of Eskimos. Hearne had lost his appetite for the mission, but he remained long enough to make a survey of the river.

After completing the survey Hearne's party started back. They crossed the frozen lakes in September and followed the caribou herds through the woods and across Point Lake and Mackay Lake. They traversed a forest region until they came to Great Slave Lake, nearly 1,000 miles west of Hudson Bay. Hearne was the first white man to see this huge body of water.

Eskimos had traded with Hudson's Bay Company ships since the
17th century.

To the south of Great Slave Lake, Hearne traveled
through country which would see the rise and develop-
ment of a powerful competitor to the Hudson's Bay Company, the North West Company.

The only copper he found, however, were some very poor specimens which eventually went to the London Museum. But he did establish beyond any reasonable doubt that no Northwest Passage existed—at least none leading out of Hudson Bay. It had been only a persistent fiction.

Hearne had explored a tremendous new area. It was the history of that vast, barren tract, so many miles from human habitation, empty of voice and footprint, that was soon to shake the Hudson's Bay Company from its long lethargy.

Samuel Hearne (left) plans Cumberland House, first of a chain of inland trading posts stretching across Canada.

Mackenzie Reaches the Pacific

The woods and lakes and streams which had echoed to the carefree chants of the *voyageurs* now rang with musket shots. The North American continent was rent by the French and Indian War. Quebec fell to the British in 1759 and Montreal, a year later. With that victory the power and the influence of the French in Canada were broken.

It seemed that the Hudson's Bay Company would have an open field. But this was not to be; in fact, they were soon to be faced with new competition as fierce as any they had ever received from the French.

New blood was about to be pumped into the northern fur trade. The Scots were coming into the picture. The clans had tried to bring Bonnie Prince Charlie to the throne of Scotland and had failed. After their bloody and decisive victory at Culloden in 1745, the English had treated the rebellious Scotsmen harshly, driving many of them to America. It was these men and their heirs, tough and hard-bitten, undeterred by a rough climate, who eventually moved out from Montreal to fill the vacuum left by the French.

These Scotsmen, joined by Englishmen and Americans, were to bring to the fur trade a new age of romance, adventure, and daring. They would explore and conquer vast new regions; they would build posts beyond the mighty

Rockies; they would cross the continent and reach the Pacific. As a result of their tenacity, furs would be carried from the mouth of the Columbia River in Oregon all the way across the continent to Montreal. From there they would find their way to Europe. In another direction, furs would be dispatched to the great markets of China.

These men began going out one at a time or in pairs to trap in the wilderness. What they earned belonged to them and not to any board of directors thousands of miles away. They were able to outdo the "Gentlemen Adventurers," for two reasons: the latter were settled in a century-old tradition; and their employees were on salary and thus had no incentive to go out into the wilds and trap.

The merchants of Montreal furnished traders supplies on credit. The traders headed west and north, very often with French veterans of earlier exploits wielding the paddles. In this great flood of men there were naturally many who were ruthless and unscrupulous. The item of trade most welcomed by the Indians was liquor.

The practice of feeding liquor to the Indians was not only regrettable, it was also dangerous. It often had such consequences as these:

In the spring of 1780, a small party of traders had been plying a band of Indians with liquor. Suddenly, one of the Indians died of natural causes. The other Indians suspected foul play. Their feelings were inflamed by drink, and they fell upon the traders, killing a number of them before they could be subdued.

There is no telling how widespread the effects of alcoholism might have become throughout the Indian tribes, or whether an Indian war might have taken place. But the Indians just then were struck by tragedy. A smallpox epidemic, said to have been carried north by a war party from

General store where furs were traded and men heard the latest news.

the Missouri River, spread from one tribe to another. Entire villages were wiped out. As the Indians fled to escape the pox, they carried it with them in every direction.

The disease killed between a third and a half of the Indian population, persisting for several years. The fur trade was brought almost to a standstill. The Montreal merchants suffered heavy losses. Ultimately, however, they did benefit

from the epidemic. It discouraged many of the more unscrupulous fly-by-night operators, leaving the trade to the
more responsible men.

There was fierce competition between the English and
the Scots as they went up the St. Lawrence. The Scots
were still burning from the way the English had treated
their clansmen after Culloden.

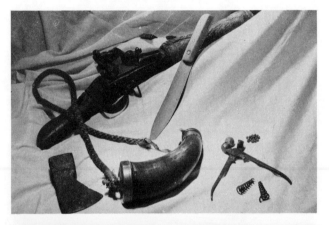

Powderhorns, axeheads,
knives, rope were prized
by Indian traders.

In contrast to the Hudson's Bay people, the Nor'Westers were eager to explore. Like the French before them, they journeyed out and broke new trails in the wilderness.

Gradually they would weld themselves together into the North West Company, the first organized competitor to the Hudson's Bay Company. One of the founders of the North West Company was Alexander Henry the Elder. (A nephew, also prominent in the fur trade, had the same name.)

Henry was born in New Jersey in 1739. During the French and Indian War he was attached to a British force. When Montreal fell in 1760, the twenty-one-year old youth received permission to go to the northern waters of the Great Lakes to trade with the Indians.

The tall, broad-shouldered, red-bearded Henry had no experience in the fur trade. He had never walked on snowshoes, he could not speak any of the Indian tongues, nor did he know how to deal with an Indian. He was equipped only with ambition and determination. But before he was through he would make history, and the great North West Company would grow as the result of his efforts.

He met disaster in his first encounter with the brawling white water of a rapids. He lost his canoes and trade goods, but was not deterred from trying again. Henry made it the next year to Michilimackinac, an island in the strait between Lake Michigan and Lake Huron. Disguising himself as a French *coureur de bois*—the Indians were still loyal to the French—Henry gradually made his way to the north shore of Lake Huron via the Ottawa and Mattawan Rivers, Lake Nipissing, and the French River. He followed Radisson's old route, the route which most of the Nor'Westers were to take in years to come.

Henry spent years in trading on Lake Superior. Then, in

1775 he moved westward. At Lake Winnipeg there occurred one of those chance meetings, so frequent in history, of gifted and determined men who would have a lasting impact on their times. Henry met burly, black-bearded Peter Pond, a seasoned veteran of the fur trade.

Pond came from Connecticut. A man of enormous physical strength, he had seen service in the French and Indian War. Later he had gone to the North country to seek his fortune. There he had gained a reputation as a shrewd, tough, and dangerous character. He was even suspected of murdering two of his Montreal rivals, who had ventured too near his trading area.

Disregarding Pond's somewhat unsavory reputation, Henry joined forces with him. At the same time the two men joined two others, the Frobisher brothers, Joseph and Thomas. And so it happened that on the far, lonely shores of Lake Winnipeg, four of the most ambitious and energetic of the Nor'Westers had come in contact.

Instead of continuing in costly competition they pooled their goods and maintained fixed prices. In his writings, Henry listed some of them. One good beaver skin would buy an Indian ten musket balls or half a pint of gunpowder. Three skins would bring a one-pound axehead; ten, a colored blanket; and twenty, a musket. Rum was still high on the list of goods desired by the Indians. But the effect on the young braves was so drastic that their chiefs were beginning to ask the traders to dilute it with water—a request Henry and his associates were only too happy to oblige.

The Frobisher brothers, an interesting pair, hailed from Yorkshire in England. They were among the few Nor'-Westers who did not come from Scotland's Highlands. Joseph Frobisher, an old hand in the North, was one of the first Englishmen to establish quarters on the Red River, in

Trader warms himself at fire.

Shooting the rapids was one of the dangers in the search for a Northwest Passage.

Manitoba. In 1774 he had built Fort La Traite on the Churchill River, seriously cutting into the trade of the Hudson's Bay Company.

Henry and the Frobishers formed their partnership in that winter of 1775 and laid the basis for an organization the methods of which would persist for forty-six years, until the North West Company merged with the Hudson's Bay Company in 1821. Carefully and skillfully they put together a monopoly which, for profit and efficiency, far exceeded anything ever achieved by their rivals on the Bay.

These were extremely courageous men, who never hesitated to take great risks in the wilderness. They were infused with the spirit of Radisson and Groseilliers. The continent was changing. Soon the guns of Concord and Lexington would herald the birth of a new nation. The British colonial society of North America was beginning to expand, extending mighty arms out across a continent. The Nor'Westers played their part in this expansion.

Henry, the Frobishers, and their associates took on a tremendous job. They were thousands of miles from Montreal, with many treacherous rivers and hostile Indian tribes between. The winters were long and punishing. Food was a constant problem.

Fur traders haggle with Indians.

But with raw muscle and unbreakable determination Henry and his associates triumphed over distance and the wilderness. Hiring French *voyageurs*—men who had worked for the old French fur traders—they moved tons of goods from the Montreal merchants north and west to their trading posts.

One of the fragile-looking thirty-foot birch canoes used in these operations was capable of accommodating a ton-and-a-half of goods in addition to food and baggage and four men. The partners' first expedition used ten such canoes. They left Lake Winnipeg and went on up the Saskatchewan. At the site of the old French post at Basquia they came upon a band of nomadic Indians led by a chief named Chatique. The Indians squatted on the ground, silently watching the white men come up from their canoes.

Chatique invited Henry and the Frobishers to his tent. After some friendly smoking and drinking the crafty Indian suddenly announced that the traders would have to make him a present of some of their goods. They hesitated. Chatique reminded them that he had more men than they did. He also reminded them that if he wished he could kill them all and take the whole of their property—so he was really being quite generous under the circumstances.

The traders had no choice. They gave Chatique three casks of gunpowder, several bags of shot and ball, two bales of tobacco, several guns, many knives, flints, and three kegs of rum.

Still fuming, the traders left the extortionist Chatique and moved on. Henry and the Frobishers pushed north toward the Churchill. From that point they could intercept Indians who were on their way downriver to trade with the Hudson's Bay Company.

Henry and his party drove on to Beaver Lake in the face of falling winter. Their food was beginning to run out. When they reached Beaver Lake, the forty-three men had food supplies for only three days. Some broke the ice over the frozen lake and fished; others hurriedly erected log cabins. All through that first long, hard winter they ate nothing but fish.

On the first of January, the inquisitive Henry set out on a journey to cross the Rocky Mountains. He got as far as the plains country. But the Indians there convinced him not to attempt the journey in winter. This daring trip was typical of Henry, for fur alone did not interest him. He was moving out into virgin territory and he was intrigued. He was filled with the spirit of the true explorer, as Radisson had been before him.

This restless curiosity, this fascination to see what lay beyond the next mountain, was characteristic of the Nor'Westers. It enabled them to open up the last frontiers of a continent, and in the process, made them wealthy.

In 1779, while the American colonies were fighting for

Sir Alexander MacKenzie became a partner in the North West Company. at 20.

independence, a crucial step was taken. Nine firms decided to pool their interests with the North West Company. The agreement was to be tried out for one year during which the entire trade beyond Lake Superior would be common property.

Some shares in the new company were held by Montreal merchants, who supplied the "wintering partners"— as the men who wintered in the interior were called—with goods. All the partners not only received a salary and a pension, but shared in the profits. It was an organization for ambitious young men who were not afraid to live in wild places and to work hard.

Soon there appeared on the scene a young Highlander who was destined to become the greatest of the Nor'Westers. In him were embodied the boundless energy, far-ranging achievements, and resolute spirit of the North West Company. He was Alexander Mackenzie.

Mackenzie was fifteen years old when he left his native Stornoway in Scotland to seek his destiny on the continent of North America. He did not linger long in Montreal, but headed straight off into the wilderness. By the time he was twenty-one, the sober, intelligent Scotsman was a partner in the North West Company. His business acumen and talents for geography had already been recognized. The men of the North West Company were not ones to let any talent go unused, and Mackenzie was to prove the most gifted of the lot.

The historian Bernard De Voto wrote of Mackenzie, "In courage, in the faculty of command, in ability to meet the unforeseen with resources of craft and skill, in the will that cannot be overborne, he has had no superior in the history of American exploration."

Spurred by the enthusiasm of Peter Pond, Mackenzie planned extensive explorations of the far North. In 1789, he was established in a post he had built on the shore of Lake Athabasca, some two hundred miles south of Great Slave Lake. Mackenzie wanted to find a river route across the continent to the Pacific.

His first expedition set forth on June 3, 1789. He was accompanied by a number of French Canadians and several Indians and their squaws. When they arrived at Great Slave Lake the ice was just beginning to break. Flowing northward out of this vast body of water was one of the largest rivers in North America—known today as the Mackenzie River.

Ever mindful of his occupation, Mackenzie established a trading post on the north side of the lake. Then he pushed westward to explore the great river. His group met strange Indians and opened the trade to them. Far to the west they saw the "wall of mountains," the snow-capped peaks of the Rockies.

Roving Indian and his squaw.

They journeyed through the wild land where the Hare Indians roamed, and then passed beyond to the land of the Quarreller tribe. Mackenzie heard fantastic tales of tribes with wings, of Indians who could kill with their staring eyes. His own Indians were frightened, but he urged them ahead. On July 10, when they were more than 1,000 miles from Lake Athabasca, Mackenzie reached the delta of the great river that today bears his name.

Mackenzie established his position at 67° 47′ N. He was both surprised and disappointed to find how far north he had traveled. It was quite evident that he was not heading for the Pacific. After going on for several days more, and paddling through the Arctic Ocean, he turned back. He returned to Lake Athabasca on September 12.

In the span of 102 days Mackenzie had traveled 3,000 miles and had mapped the second longest river in North America. But he remained dissatisfied, persisting in his yearning to reach the Pacific.

Mackenzie felt himself deficient in the sciences of astronomy and navigation. He left Athabasca and went to England. There he spent the winter of 1791–92 studying, and obtaining the necessary instruments, including star tables, a sextant, and a chronometer.

On May 9, 1793 he set out again in search of the Pacific Ocean. But first he completed trade agreements in the Athabasca area—Mackenzie never neglected the fur trade.

The long journey could not have been made without great daring and sacrifice. With grim determination he led his expedition against swift, foaming rivers, rugged mountains, and hostile Indians. Unable to negotiate the swirling waters of the Peace River, his men carried their canoes for seven miles through forest and over mountains.

When they put their craft into water again, the slash-

A trapper looking for game.

ing savage water destroyed them. They built others. Nothing was going to stop Mackenzie. He described the Peace River as "one sheet of tumbling water," and noted that it was rough enough to frighten even the veteran *voyageurs* and Indian hunters who were accompanying him.

They went on and met Indians who had never seen white men. Mackenzie questioned them all, learning about the various waterways, about the great ocean that lay beyond. On June 12 he crossed the Continental Divide and entered streams that seemed to be flowing backward. They were bound for the Pacific.

Mackenzie's men rebelled. He advised them that they could turn back and that he would continue alone. Awed by this display of courage and iron determination, the men remained. Finally on July 20, "at about eight" o'clock in the morning, Mackenzie wrote: "we got out of the river, which discharges itself by various channels into an arm of the sea."

He had done it. The dream of countless men, the dream of crossing the North American continent, had been achieved. Mackenzie had sailed down the Bella Coola River, through Dean Channel, and out to the Pacific Ocean, at a point approximately one hundred miles north of Vancouver Island.

With great pride he wrote on a rock-bluff in the channel, "Alexander Mackenzie, from Canada, by land, the twenty-second of July, one thousand seven hundred and ninety-three."

These words, written with vermilion mixed in melted grease, signaled the achievement of the Northwest Passage—but by land, not by sea.

Mackenzie went back to his point of departure on Peace River. The return journey was upstream with many uphill portages. It proved to be a difficult ordeal. Soon after, in 1801, he sailed to London. Upon publication of the account of his exploration in his journal he was immediately lionized. In 1802 he was knighted by King George III in recognition of his achievement.

Massacre at Seven Oaks

In spite of the Hudson's Bay Company's moves to expand, the North West Company continued to outdo them. One reason was Hudson's Bay's practice of giving their employees a bonus for every skin purchased—regardless of the price paid for the skin. This proved costly to the company. The North West Company, on the other hand, made partners of their qualified men. In effect the company was owned by its employees: everyone had an equal stake in it. This virtually insured greater efficiency.

The North West Company continued to expand. Not content with its holdings in the rich Athabasca region, it was now carrying the trade across the Rockies. Beaver were becoming scarce in the East, for in 1804 an epidemic had seriously depleted the beaver population. This affected Hudson's Bay more than it did their rivals, for the North West men were spread far and wide across the fur country.

Indians sometimes massacred visiting traders.

With inefficiency slowly strangling it, in 1804 the Hudson's Bay Company was willing to sell out to the Nor'-Westers, and by 1809 the company was on the verge of bankruptcy. Alexander Mackenzie was ready in 1810 to buy out Hudson's Bay. But his partners saw no need of it— the "Gentlemen Adventurers" were no longer a serious threat.

However, a new man of dynamic character was about to

take control of the Hudson's Bay Company. He was
Thomas Douglas, the Earl of Selkirk. Selkirk was a Scotsman who dreamed of colonizing the Canadian plains with
his Highland countrymen, so many of whom were now
destitute. Using the Hudson's Bay Company as a means of
realizing his dream, Selkirk invested heavily in the company. By 1811 he was in virtual control.

Selkirk was a stubborn man, convinced of the wisdom of
his ways. But he was also a man of great sincerity, with a
genuine desire to help his less fortunate countrymen. He
took title to 110,000 square miles of land which the Nor'-
Westers considered their private domain. Selkirk's tract
included parts of what is now Manitoba in Canada and
Minnesota and North Dakota in the United States. Here
he intended to establish an agricultural settlement.

It was important to Selkirk's plan that the Hudson's Bay
Company be invigorated and made to operate at a profit.
He revamped the company's business procedures along the
lines of the North West Company, giving his employees a
one-half share of net profits. For the first time in its 140-
year history, the employees of the company had a vested
interest in its success.

Selkirk's philanthropic idea was resented by the Nor'-
Westers. His 110,000 acres included the most fertile land
of the Red River Valley, where the buffalo herds wintered.
These herds were a prime source of food for the trappers
in the area. It was feared that agricultural activity of great
magnitude would chase the beaver from their streams, as
well as drive away the buffalo.

In spite of Selkirk's ability and experience, however, his
scheme for colonizing the Canadian plains was doomed to
failure. A colony in the middle of the continent was at that
time 1,000 miles from the nearest outpost of civilization.

Buffalo herds in the Red River Valley were a source of food to trappers.

How the colonists would dispose of their agricultural products was a logistics problem Selkirk had obviously not faced.

What frightened the Nor'Westers was the fact that even though Selkirk's grand scheme could not work, he was accomplishing something else that had never been done before—bringing the Hudson's Bay Company out of its conservatism. The company would soon be establishing outposts in the far country and rehabilitating itself in the fur trade.

With Selkirk claiming complete control over his land—land which the North West Company had roamed over and monopolized for over forty years—the situation became tense.

In 1816 Selkirk ordered the North West Company to quit "his lands." He instructed his agents to treat the men of the rival company as poachers. He forbade them to cut timber or to kill buffalo from horseback. To aim such a proclamation at men who had conquered a wilderness and were now living off it was the same as bringing fire to dynamite. Selkirk had made a mistake in taking the colonists to central Canada, and now he was compounding that mistake with high-handed proclamations. Violence was inevitable.

It finally broke loose on the Red River, in the summer of 1816. Some sixty half-breeds under the command of Cuthbert Grant of the North West Company were riding toward the cabins of some settlers when they were intercepted by the Hudson's Bay Company governor, Robert Semple.

Semple had only twenty-seven men with him. He ordered them to stop. Taunts were exchanged, then harsh words. Grant's men opened fire. The Hudson's Bay men were badly outnumbered. A brief, bloody, one-sided battle took place. Semple and twenty of his men were killed in a fight. Though Grant tried to prevent it he could not control his followers. Only one of the half-breeds was killed.

The Seven Oaks massacre made both sides realize that a repetition of such violence would prove disastrous to both parties. All concerned agreed that it must cease. The North West Company, for one, had other problems to face. At about the same time Lord Selkirk had entered the fur trade picture, John Jacob Astor, an immigrant from Germany, was establishing his Pacific Fur Company.

After the beaver epidemic of 1804 had made the precious animal scarce, the North West Company recognized the necessity of expanding their trade still further. About

Astor planned to open up the fur trade on the Pacific coast.

this time, Astor was planning to open the trade on the
Pacific coast. He offered the Nor'Westers a one-third interest if they joined him. They refused and he went it alone.

Astor dispatched two parties to the Pacific coast. One
went by sea on the 300-ton barque *Tonquin* under the
command of Jonathan Thorn, a veteran of the United
States Navy. The other followed the Lewis and Clark trail
overland under Wilson Price Hunt. Thorn brought his ship
into the mouth of the Columbia River in March, 1811, and
set to work building the trading post that would be named
Astoria.

In the summer of 1811, Thorn took the *Tonquin* and its
twenty-three man crew to Nootka, on the west coast of
Vancouver Island. There, the trade was most profitable. At
Nootka, Thorn made the mistake of permitting a great

Indians swarmed aboard the *Tonquin* to pillage.

many Indians to board his ship. The Indians concealed knives and clubs in their furs. At a signal, they attacked the traders, killing all but one of the crew, who remained in hiding aboard the ship.

The next day the Indians came swarming aboard to pillage the *Tonquin's* rich cargo. The crewman slipped down to the powder room and, when the deck was filled with Indians, touched off a blast which blew up the ship, himself included. Washington Irving reconstructed the scene this way:

Arms and legs and mutilated bodies were blown into the air, and dreadful havoc was made in the surrounding canoes. The bay presented an awful spectacle after the catastrophe. The ship had disappeared. Upwards of a hundred savages were destroyed, many more shockingly mutilated, and for days afterwards the limbs and bodies of the slain were thrown upon the beach.

In spite of setbacks such as the *Tonquin* disaster, Astor's men went vigorously to work. Parties traveled up the Columbia and built posts on the sites of what are today Salem and Spokane, in Oregon. They even went far to the North, making contact with Russian traders in the country the Indians called *Alakh-Skhah,* which meant "great land."

The North West Company, unhappy with Astor's plans, decided to take advantage of the outbreak of war in 1812. Aided by a British man-of-war which reached the Columbia in November, 1813, the Nor'Westers took over Astoria, in northwest Oregon. They renamed it Fort George.

When the treaty of peace was signed in 1815, its terms returned Astoria to America, but the Nor'Westers remained in possession. The energetic Nor'Westers had built posts up and down the Columbia River and were shipping directly to China. They also sent trading parties down the coast, probably as far south as California.

Just as the North West Company was expanding to a greater extent than ever, the Hudson's Bay Company decided to become adventurous. They really had little choice. The scarcity of beaver had hit Hudson's Bay harder than the Nor'Westers because of their limited field of operations. So in 1815, Selkirk began sending men into the lucrative areas of the Peace and Athabasca, in northern Alberta.

The old rivalry between the companies turned intense and bitter. A Hudson's Bay party going hungry on the Peace River was denied food by the Nor'Westers. Eight of the men starved to death as a result.

Aside from that one incident, by scattering the game and inducing the Indians to keep away from the Hudson's Bay men, the North West Company successfully defended their trade that first winter. The Nor'Westers were equally successful in shutting their competitors out of the trade throughout the entire Mackenzie basin.

In the summer of 1818, however, a party of Hudson's

Bay men, under the command of Colin Robertson, succeeded in erecting a fort near Smoky Forks. This was a
strategic position from which they could command the
lucrative Peace River trade.

The achievement irked the North West Company men.
There followed an almost comic sequence of events.
Whenever opportunity arose, each side arrested men of the
opposition, claiming the sanction of legal warrants. The
comedy took a tragic turn, though, with the arrest of Ben-
jamin Frobisher, son of Joseph Frobisher, one of the original Nor'Westers.

Ben Frobisher was a bruising man of violent temper.
When the Hudson's Bay people tried to arrest him at Lake
Winnipeg, Frobisher fought back with the fury of a grizzly.
It took several men to subdue him. During the melee Fro-
bisher suffered a severe head injury.

Frobisher was taken to York Factory and jailed. He
finally escaped and tried to cut through the wilderness to
the nearest North West outpost. But he perished on the
way—from his injuries, according to the North West
people.

Frobisher's death roused the hatred of the Nor'Westers
to an even greater pitch. Both sides intensified their hostile
tactics. Canoe parties were intercepted and men arrested.
Grudges became fierce and duels were fought. Traders
and canoemen alike went heavily armed, ready to shoot
to kill.

The hostilities in Canada aroused the wrath of Great
Britain, for in 1817 His Majesty's government had issued
a proclamation forbidding violence. That proclamation
was being ignored.

The situation came to a head in the winter of 1820. A
young clerk named George Simpson, who had been hired

Sir George Simpson brought peace between rival fur trading companies.

by Hudson's Bay, arrived at Lake Athabasca. Simpson was both tenacious and diplomatic. He brought a peaceful influence to the warring companies, at a time when England was finally beginning to take an active part in the hostility between the two rivals which dominated the Canadian fur trade.

At the time of Simpson's negotiations, the Governor General of Canada sent W. B. Coltman to the Far West to investigate the differences between the companies. Coltman was an impartial observer. He spoke to men of both sides, including Selkirk and the principal Nor'Westers. Coltman saw that both sides were adamant. On his return, he filed a confidential report saying that unless a merger could be arranged between the companies there would be no peace in the vast, rich wilderness.

Nothing was done immediately, but Simpson's soothing influence was beginning to be felt. The death of Lord Selkirk in 1820 removed the last serious stumbling block to a compromise. By way of exerting pressure to bring about a solution, Parliament offered to grant a lease to the united company. This would give it exclusive fur trade rights to all Canada, excluding only the eastern provinces and the land granted Hudson's Bay under its original charter of 1670.

The agreement to merge was signed on March 26, 1821. The two companies united under the venerable name of the Hudson's Bay Company. The long, costly battle of the fur trade across the rivers, lakes, plains, and mountains of Canada was over at last.

British fur traders receive surrender of Fort Astoria.

Trappers of the Western States

John Jacob Astor was the greatest of the American fur traders. He was born on July 17, 1763, in the village of Waldorf, near Heidelburg, Germany. His father was a butcher, but the ambitious young man disappointed him by not taking up that vocation. Instead, at the age of seventeen, he went to London and two years later, sailed to America.

Almost immediately after arriving in America in 1784, young Astor entered the fur trade. He soon earned a reputation as a shrewd and intelligent trader.

Astor's early purchases were made from the North West Company at Montreal. He made such handsome profits when he resold these furs in the United States or in Europe that he decided to strike out on his own. With the enthusiastic cooperation and approval of President Jefferson, Astor set out to exploit the Far West fur trade. The great explorers Lewis and Clark had noted the fur trade possibilities while crossing the continent to the Pacific.

In 1809 Astor established the American Fur Company, with a capital of one million dollars. Within two years he was making plans to control the trade of the entire American territory. His ambition was to build posts along the Missouri and Columbia Rivers, with headquarters at the mouth of the Columbia. Astor envisioned his fur-laden

John Jacob Astor crushed competition by paying Indians more for furs.

ships trading at what was then one of the great fur markets at Canton, China, and returning with goods from the Orient.

Astor's only serious competitor early in the American trade was a man named Manuel Lisa. He was born in America of Spanish parents. Lisa was trying to control all of the upper Missouri trade. In 1807 he went up the Missouri, and then the Yellowstone, until he reached the mouth of the Big Horn, in Montana. There he established a small trading post. He organized his Missouri Fur Company in 1808.

Lisa's trappers were continually running into hostility from the powerful Blackfeet. The tribe resented any white men entering their domain, part of which today is Yellowstone National Park.

One of Lisa's best trappers was John Colter, who was to undergo an experience that would make him a legend in the history of the West. Captured by Blackfeet, Colter was stripped naked and told to start running. For their own amusement, the Indians had decided to give him a sporting chance before sending their fastest runners to catch him and kill him.

The barefoot Colter ran across rocks and cactus, through thorny brush, up and down hills. He ran for six miles. One by one his howling, hatchet-waving pursuers collapsed. One finally caught up to him. They fought and Colter killed him with the Indian's spear. Colter then dove into the Three Forks River and hid under driftwood while the angry Blackfeet searched for him. Seven days later he staggered into Lisa's post on the Big Horn.

Lisa's ambitions did not extend to the West coast, but John Jacob Astor's did. With the declaration of war between England and America in 1812, the Nor'Westers moved upon the Americans at Astoria. Badly outnumbered, separated by 3,000 miles from their source of supplies, the Astorians yielded without a struggle.

In spite of the American victory in the War of 1812, Astor did not get his trade rights back. A law passed by Congress in 1815 forbade British traders from operating on American soil. But just what constituted American soil in the case of the Oregon boundaries remained undefined. Although this situation eliminated the American Fur Company from the west coast, all trading posts east of the Rockies passed into the possession of Americans, or more specifically, of Astor.

By the shrewd practice of hiring former North West Company men Astor was able to establish a monopoly east of the Rockies quite rapidly and thoroughly. He was able to crush most competitors by the simple expedient of paying the Indians exorbitant prices for their furs.

Astor gradually bought up and absorbed any competition he could not crush, including the American interests of the North West Company. Manuel Lisa died in 1820. Astor moved in on the Missouri valley trade at once and established the western division of his American Fur Company at St. Louis.

In 1831 the American Fur Company went into the Wyoming beaver fields, particularly around the Green and Wind Rivers. Here, however, the company found itself in direct competition with its only serious rival, the Rocky Mountain Fur Company.

Two St. Louis fur merchants, William Ashley and Andrew Henry, had launched a partnership that eventually became the Rocky Mountain Fur Company. By employing the most skilled trappers, including such famed mountain men as Jim Bridger, Bill Sublette, and Jedediah Smith, the

Manuel Lisa founded the Missouri Fur Company.

new company was able to score impressive successes in the American trade.

Ashley and Henry sent their trappers out into the wilds. To systematize their operations they arranged for a rendez-vous to be held once a year at an appointed place. At that time, supplies were brought to the trappers and their furs were collected. These rendezvous have become part of the folklore of the West; they were annual holidays for the men of the lonely mountains.

The trappers straggled in one and two at a time to the annual get-together, eager to obtain ammunition, tobacco, whisky, new traps, and other supplies, and to enjoy a little human companionship after their months of solitude in the woods. The Indians also attended, bringing their furs to trade for beads, bright blankets, mirrors, and other prod-ucts of the white man's factories.

Before the trading came several days of pure, unin-hibited roughhouse fun. There was horse-racing and tar-get-shooting and heavy drinking and brawling and the pursuit of Indian maidens.

Alfred Jacob Miller, who attended the July, 1837, ren-dezvous at Green River, Wyoming, left this description of the event:

The first day is devoted to "High Jinks," in which feasting, drinking and gambling form prominent parts. Sometimes an Indian becomes so excited with "Fire Water" that he com-mences "running a muck"—he is pursued, thrown or knocked down, and secured, in order to keep him from mischief. "Affairs of honor" now and then are adjusted between rival trappers— one of the parties, of course, receiving a complete drubbing;— all caused evidently from mixing too much alcohol with their water. Night closes this scene of revelry and confusion. The fol-lowing days exhibit the strongest contrast to this. The Fur Companys' great tent is raised;—the Indians erect their picturesque white lodges;—the accumulated furs of the hunting season are brought forth, and the Company's tent is a besieged and busy place.

These trappers were a rugged crew. For many of them the annual rendezvous was the first time in a year they would see another white man. One of their contemporaries wrote of their life in the open air: "Their rifles furnished them with food and they slept under the stars without shelter, enjoying perfect health in the pure mountain air, and were never so happy as when fraternizing with, or fighting, Indians."

In 1831 the Rocky Mountain Fur Company's monopoly on the lush Wyoming beaver country was challenged by Astor's American Fur Company. Two of Astor's men, Vanderburgh and Drips, began trailing the Rocky Mountain men in hopes of discovering the precise locations of their valuable trapping grounds.

Rocky Mountain trappers cut loose at their annual "rendezvous."

Tom Fitzpatrick and Jim Bridger led the Astor men on a merry chase through the mountains. The wily mountain men took their pursuers into the country of the murderous Blackfeet. Suddenly Vanderburgh was killed in an Indian ambush. In another ambush, Bridger himself took two arrowheads in his back. He carried one of them for three years until Doctor Marcus Whitman, the famous American physician, removed it for him.

After 1832 the American Fur Company moved full force into the Rocky Mountain domain and fierce, ruthless competition began. The competition led to murder and stealing. It could not go on for long, however. Though the Rocky Mountain people had the more skilled trappers, Astor's company was richer and able to pay more for furs and sell goods more cheaply.

In 1834 Astor, now over seventy years old, retired. He sold out his interests to a St. Louis firm that agreed to maintain the name, American Fur Company. The new management made overtures to the Rocky Mountain Company. The fur trade of the United States and its western territories was consolidated into one huge combine.

Again the beaver trade had been the spearhead of exploration and discovery, as it had been since the days of Champlain and Radisson. Seeking the hapless animal's abode, the trappers of the Rocky Mountain Company—the "Mountain Men" of Western history and folklore—did their share in opening the West. They were the first to see the sources of the Yellowstone, the Green, the Platte, and the Snake Rivers. Jedediah Smith led the first expedition of white men into California from the Great Salt Lake. So far as is known, Smith was also the first white man to travel up the Pacific coast from San Francisco to the Columbia River.

Mountain men who explored the west seeking beaver were a rugged crew.

The Last Frontier

Now began the Hudson's Bay Company's golden age.
Under the skillful direction of George Simpson, the company (now merged with the North West Company)
reached its greatest heights. Using the extensive trade and
travel facilities at his disposal, Simpson built a chain of
trading forts extending from the Bay, across the prairies
and on out to the Pacific coast.

In the summer of 1824, Simpson set out for a visit to the
Columbia River. After an arduous journey of eighty-four
days—from York Factory to Fort George—Simpson arrived on the west coast. It was his intention to make the
trade west of the Rockies as profitable as possible. He saw
to it that forts were built at the mouth of the Fraser River
and, later, just south of Russian Alaska.

Simpson also appointed three of the company's best
men, John McLoughlin, Peter Ogden, and Samuel Black,
to take command in the West. McLoughlin, a doctor by
training, was the most colorful of the three. Simpson wrote
of him: "He was such a figure as I should not like to meet in
a dark night in one of the bye lanes in the neighborhood of
London, dressed in clothes that had once been fashionable,
but now covered with a thousand patches of different
colors; his beard would do honor to the chin of a grizzly
bear."

Simpson feared that a boundary settlement might give the Americans rights to Fort George. In 1825 he built Fort Vancouver at Belle Vue Point, putting McLoughlin in charge. Belle Vue Point was about seventy-five miles from the mouth of the Columbia. Simpson was confident he would retain the trade of the Chinooks and other Indians in the area. Fort Vancouver became the seat of the company's coastal operations; its bustling activity convinced Simpson that the Columbia trade would reap handsome rewards.

McLoughlin decided to concentrate his fur-hunting expeditions on the southern side of the river, where the American trappers were most active. With the boundary line still undecided and McLoughlin apprehensive lest the decision eventually go against the British, he was told by the shrewd Simpson to send men south of the river, "as while we have access thereto it is in our interest to reap all the advantage we can for ourselves, and leave it in as bad a state as possible for our successors."

George Simpson built Fort Vancouver as a trading post at Belle Vue Point.

McLoughlin sent trapping parties led by Ogden into the
Snake River country. Although these parties barely made
a profit it was Simpson's intention to keep trapping there,
"as the more we impoverish the country the less likelihood
is there of our being assailed by opposition."

While the Hudson's Bay men were competing with the
American trappers south of the Columbia, the company
was also looking northward. Here they competed with the
Russian American Company. Although there were American trading ships plying the coast, they were less threaten-
ing than the Russians because the latter were making territorial claims.

The Russian company had been granted exclusive trading rights on the coast north of 55° in 1799. This gave it
clear territorial claims. The Russians built a post at Sitka,
later rebuilding it as New Archangel. They also built Fort
Ross (originally Fort Russki) on Bodega Bay, about fifty
miles north of where the city of San Francisco stands today. There were no problems until the early 1820s, when
the Hudson's Bay Company, led by Simpson, decided to
expand its trade to the coast.

The Russo-American convention of 1824 and the Anglo-
Russian convention of 1825 won for the British and Americans access to the coast and inland waters of the Russian
company.

But when the British and the Americans finally did enter
the hitherto exclusively Russian hunting grounds, there
was little actual conflict, since they were primarily inter-
ested in beaver. The Russians, on the other hand, were
trading mainly in seals and sea otters.

Simpson and McLoughlin seized the opportunity to expand the coastal trade on behalf of Hudson's Bay. To
achieve this end they would have to compete with Amer-

ican traders. By building a post at the Nass River and back-
ing it with solidly organized shipping, Simpson believed
they would be able to drive out the American competition
in two or three years.

With the Americans out of the picture, Simpson hoped
also to take over the business of supplying the Russians
with products from the United Kingdom, in addition to the
pork, beef, and grain raised in Vancouver. But after much
delay, the Russians rejected Simpson's proposal.

Nevertheless the British went ahead with their plan to
assume control of the coastal trade. Simpson sent a relative,
Aemilius Simpson, in command of several ships to the Nass
River to choose a site for operations. By the summer of
1831 the post, Fort Simpson, had been established at a
narrow channel seven miles up river.

The British then proceeded to follow the American ships
with their own. They sought to drive the Americans from
the trade by outbidding them. In order to do this, they had
to violate their own proscription against trading liquor and
guns to the Indians. It was always perilous and unwise to
trade this way, but when competition entered the trade
good judgment very often waned.

In 1835 the British introduced a steamer, the *Beaver*, to
the waters of the fur trade. The vessel so greatly impressed
the Indians that it won for Hudson's Bay much of the trade
that had been going to the Americans and the Russians.
The *Beaver* could ply the coast with ease. It did not depend on the wind, and could be counted on to average
thirty miles a day. The fur trade, which had begun with
intrepid men going down the St. Lawrence in light birch-
bark canoes, continued across the continent, with squat,
dependable steamers plowing the icy waters of the north
Pacific.

In boats like these trappers plied lakes and streams in the 19th century.

The Hudson's Bay men were not through exploring. In 1838 an expedition headed by Thomas Simpson, another relative of the famous George, and Peter Dease plunged into the wilderness. The party left from Great Bear Lake, in what is now the Northwest Territory of Canada. They proceeded to the Coppermine River and then eastward along the coast as far as Cape Beaufort. They discovered the large, uninhabited island known today as Victoria and, further east, King William Island.

Dease and Thomas Simpson, employees of Hudson's
Bay, were in the great tradition of such other trader-ex-
plorers as Radisson, Henry Kelsey, Anthony Hendry, and
Alexander Mackenzie.

In 1839 the British and Russian governments came to
an agreement whereby the Russian American Company
granted the Hudson's Bay Company a ten-year lease of the
coast and inland country between Cape Spencer and lati-

Indians were for the most part friendly, but sometimes attacked
traders.

tude 54° 40′. The British were to pay a rental of 2,000 otter skins a year. These exclusive rights gave the Hudson's Bay Company a powerful economic advantage over the Americans in the competition for the coastal trade.

But this advantage was becoming increasingly slim. The fur harvest was dropping rapidly, year by year. From the St. Lawrence to the lakes, from the Bay across the continent to the coast, the beaver was being trapped out. Broken dams lay unrepaired and streams flowed over forgotten or abandoned traps rusting in the water. And the gloomy trappers were telling tales of the silk hat. In London and New York and Montreal men were discarding their beaver hats and hurrying to buy silk, to keep up with the new style.

Trading in furs continued to be the chief source of income of the Hudson's Bay Company until 1867. In that year its vast land holdings under the charter were given back to the British crown. The crown in turn ceded it to be incorporated in the Canadian Confederation, which came into being at that time.

Since those days the fur trade has changed and is still changing out of all recognition. Women, rather than men, have become the prime market for furs. Synthetic fibers, which can be made cheaply from oil and coal, are cutting into the market for animal furs.

Two-thirds of the skins used today are taken from animals raised on fur farms in the United States, Canada, and elsewhere.

But that remaining third is still trapped—trapped by men who still use many of the trails and routes that were discovered by Radisson and Groseilliers and the numerous, nameless *voyageurs* and *coureurs de bois* who came before and after them.

"I took ye for an Injun."

Other echoes of the past remain. This year and every year, the fur auction is held in the great Beaver Hall on the banks of the Thames in London, just as it has been since Radisson's time. In 1964, the last year for which figures are available, 27 million pounds sterling (about 75 million dollars) worth of furs were sold there.

Meanwhile, after centuries of being harried and hunted, the industrious little beaver has come into his own. Cherished by farmers as a water conservationist because of his unique dam-building ability, he is allowed to go about his business in peace, helping to preserve such bits of the great primeval wilderness as still remain to us.

BIBLIOGRAPHY

Atherton, Lewis Eldon, *The Pioneer Merchants in Mid America.*

Davidson, Gordon Charles, *Northwest Company.*

Dalrymple, Alexander, *Plan for Promoting the Fur-Trade and Securing it to this Country by Uniting the Operations of the East India and Hudson's Bay Companies.*

De Voto, Bernard A., *Across the Missouri.*

Encyclopedia of Canada, W. Stewart Wallace, ed.

Heaton, Herbert, *A History of Trade and Commerce with Special Reference to Canada.*

Innis, Harold A., *The Fur Trade in Canada.*

Jeffreys, Charles William, *Canada's Past in Pictures.*

—, *The Picture Gallery of Canadian History.*

Johnson, Eda Amanda, *Michigan Fur Traders.*

Jones, Evan, and Dale L. Morgan, *Trappers and Mountain Men.*

Kellogg, L. P., *French Regime in Wisconsin.*

Kelly, Charles, *Old Greenwood: The Story of Caleb Greenwood; Trapper, Pathfinder, and Early Pioneer.*

Larpenteur, Charles, *Forty Years a Fur Trader on the Upper Missouri.*

Laut, Agnes Christina, *The Adventures of England on the Hudson Bay.*

—, *Fur Trade of America.*

—, *Heralds of Empire; Being the Story of One Ramsay Stanhope, Lieutenant to Pierre Radisson in Northern Fur.*

Rich, Edwin Ernest, *History of the Hudson's Bay Company.*

INDEX